Stonehenge
Solving the Neolithic Universe

Expanded edition

By Jonathan Morris

FRONT MATTER

Copyright © Jonathan M. Morris
© MMXIII

All rights reserved. All images, photographs and other image types copyright of the author or others. Except for the quotation of brief passages in criticism, no part of this publication may be reproduced, stored in a retrieval system, or transmitted, in any form or by any means, electronic, mechanical, photocopying, recording or otherwise, without the prior permission of the publishers. The Author asserts his moral right to be identified as the author of this work. Some portions of this work patent pending and/or other forms of registration. Definitions and meanings of patents, designs and copyright described above should be understood in accordance with the laws of the United Kingdom. The following discussion is intended to help explain historical coincidences relative to various new inventions. The author is not an archaeological or historical expert and it should be appreciated that the discussion is not an acknowledgment or admission that any of the material referred to was or has been part of the common general knowledge in the United Kingdom or elsewhere as at the time of writing. 'Solving the Neolithic Universe' ™ is a trademark of this series of books. Front cover image courtesy of NASA.

www.stonehinge.co.uk

Original First edition (electronic) published November 11, 2012, Eastbourne, UK
Published by Handow (Hanwell & Dowling) Publishing using the Createspace and Kindle platforms under ISBN numbers 978-1481876353 and/or 148187635X

www.handow.co.uk

This expanded edition first published at the Autumn Equinox, 2013
Edition 2.1

ISBN of this edition:
ISBN-13: 978-1492736882
ISBN-10: 1492736880

ACKNOWLEDGEMENTS

For Inspiration
I would like to thank the following authors:
Aubrey Burl, Rodney Castleden, Christopher Chippindale, Rosamund M J Cleal, FE Halliday, Gerald S Hawkins, Rosemary Hill, Anthony Johnson, Jean-Pierre Mohen, R Montague, Mike Parker Pearson, Mark Pendergrast, Mike Pitts, F Pryor, Julian Richards, J M Roberts, Lewis Spence & K E Walker.
And, especially, Wikipedia.

In particular, this book would not have been possible without Anthony Johnson's book: 'Solving Stonehenge', Professor Parker Pearson's book: 'Stonehenge: Exploring the Greatest Stone Age Mystery' and the English Heritage book 'Stonehenge in its Landscape'.

Engineering and solar concepts in The Broken Stone were expanded upon in various discussions within the Megalithic Portal Forum, whose contributors kindly offered advice and criticism. This introduction summarizes the concepts behind some of those discussions. In particular, I would like to thank George Currie and Neil Wiseman for their input into Chapter 2.

I am in debt to NASA, Neil Wiseman, Terence Meaden and CIBSE for kindly creating and/or supplying some of the images for this extended edition.

FOREWORD

The images in the following text were produced using a three dimensional computer model of a newly invented renewable energy device. This was the device which was later found to replicate the stones at Stonehenge as they may have been when first constructed. In addition to working as a solar concentrator, this new invention can also be used to create a miniature version of the Universe assuming that the world is fixed at the centre.

Every feature of Stonehenge is shown to be explainable using a very old, and little known, way of scientific thinking combined with engineering principles. This introduction describes how the search for knowledge could have resulted in an early fundamental view of the Universe and the subsequent creation of Stonehenge itself.

Stonehenge's plan layout will be shown to be the same as an idealised geocentric description of our Universe. Its inner stone monument is demonstrated to be capable of producing a spectacular public display of solar movement. The arrangement of this system is shown to be based on a simple method of tracking celestial objects.

This type of description of the Universe is almost identical to the same ideas produced in Ancient Greece some two thousand years later; when Ptolemy, Plato and Aristotle were to discover how their Universe worked.

However, Ancient Greece does not credit Grecians with this discovery. Instead, a mysterious and obscure Titan, known as Hyperion, is credited. Little is known about him and there is little to no reference to Hyperion during the War of the Titans. Similar myths, telling of a great war, exist throughout Europe and the Near East: One generation of Gods, or perhaps tribes, oppose those in power to win out the day.

Whoever *or whatever* he was, he was perhaps too far away from Greece to be involved.

> *Of Hyperion we are told that he was the first to understand, by diligent attention and observation, the movement of both the sun and the moon and the other stars, and the seasons as well, in that they are caused by these bodies, and to make these facts known to others; and that for this reason he was called the father of these bodies, since he had begotten, so to speak, the speculation about them and their nature.'*
> Diodorus Siculus, Library of History 5.67.

This book is of 6 parts:

The Introduction describes what Stonehenge is, and its history.

Part 1 shows how Stonehenge's plan layout is the same as an idealized geocentric description of the Universe. Its inner stone monument is shown to be capable of producing a spectacular public display of solar movement. Rather than presenting a fully referenced document, this introduction is based on a series of diagrams which, hopefully, will be easy to understand.

Part 2 shows how and where an early knowledge of the Universe could have been obtained. It also shows that, in all the locations needed, the monuments of that period appear to fit with this type of enquiry into the nature of the Universe.

Part 3 is about how the monuments would be perceived: It shows how mythological and Arthurian references also appear to fit this explanation of Stonehenge and other monuments. This part offers an explanation for the Grail and the Four Treasures of the Tuatha Dé Danann.

Part 4 is a summary of parts 1 to 3.

Part 5 contains an epilogue and some appendices with explanations of some aspects of Astronomy and technical detail on spherical solar collectors and some test experiments.

Part 6 contains notes, references, an index and a list of illustrations.

Contents

1: AN INTRODUCTION TO STONEHENGE 1
The people 2
The path to Stonehenge 4
Stonehenge: The word 6
A history of discovery 8
A potted history of the monument's phases 12
The Stones: A potted summary 21
The axis of the monument 25
Metals & Stonehenge 27
New Evidence 29
Theories 32
2: STONEHENGE AND THE HINGE 34
The times 35
Astronomy on a fixed world 36
The Hinge of the Heavens 43
A special device in a geocentric Universe 52
The three season device 57
Decay 65
Summary 66
3: THE SIZE OF THE WORLD 67
The idea 68
Finding a hill's height 69
A modern experiment 76
Calculating the size of the world 78
The rotation of the Heavens 81
Summary 84
4: FOLKLORE 85
The Grail 85
Treasures of the Tuatha Dé Danann 88
The Druids 89
Summary 90
5: THE UNIVERSE 91
Coincidences: Part 1 93
Coincidences: Part 2 95
Summary 103
6: EPILOGUE 105
APPENDIX A: The rotation of our planet 107
Some technical stuff 109
Apparent solar planes 110
APPENDIX B: Spherical solar collectors 113
Background 114
Theory 115
Before Stonehenge 119
NOTES & REFERENCES 127
References 140
INDEX 143
Illustrations 148

1: AN INTRODUCTION TO STONEHENGE

Stonehenge is one of a thousand or so stone circles within the British Isles. Similar circles also exist in some parts of Northern Europe. But a henge is a circular structure, more usually an enclosure, and is quite peculiar to Britain.[01,02] Surprisingly, Stonehenge is not a henge.

Nevertheless, Stonehenge is a truly exceptional circle: It is one of the few monuments in Britain where megaliths were carved to shape.[03] Huge stone lintels, weighing 5-6 tons[04] and locked together with joints similar to those found in woodworking,[05] were placed onto massive 25 ton[04] sarsen stones to make a giant 30 metre (≈100') internally facing[06] ring of stone.

Inside the ring, even larger stones weighing up to 40 tons, with lintels up to 16 tons,[07] were laid out in a horse-shoe pattern which points north east in the direction of the summer solstice sunrise. The tallest of these stones would have been about five times higher than the average person.

Stonehenge: As seen from north east

The people

Four and a half thousand years ago, the people were very much like the inhabitants of modern Britain: Some 85% of the genes in today's white Britons are directly descended from the early hunter-gatherer groups who thrived, and moved ever northwards, as the glaciers of the last ice-age retreated.[11]

But at Stonehenge, the people were not all from the local area: At nearby Boscombe Down, the burials are known to be of people who had come from Wales or the Lake District.[12]

Not only were the people not all local, but some were not even born in Britain: The richest burial of the time was of a man who died aged 35-45 years, and is known as the 'Amesbury Archer'. Analysis shows that he died some time between 2200-2400BC and came from Central Europe.[13] Copper, in one of his knives, is known to come from Spain. No-one knows what caused him to come to Britain, nor why his possessions came from so far away: This island, once part of mainland Europe, had become isolated from the mainland some three thousand years earlier.

But the Amesbury Archer was only the start of this migration.[14] Something special was going on in Britain: Cross-channel trade was starting to develop and, in the later middle Bronze age, would expand on a much larger scale.[15] People were coming to this island from far and wide. At some point later, another great wave of people came from the Atlantic seaboard[16] to settle in Ireland, Scotland and the west of England.

Though life was hard compared to modern times, the population was small and had access to ample natural resources. Clothing was made of fur, leather and vegetable fibres such as flax (linen).[17] Although simply made, it is possible that some clothes of that era would not look out of place today.

Surrounding Stonehenge, a partially wooded landscape, with small arable plots and large areas of grass, provided both grain for the people and grazing for livestock.[18] Grown during their warm summers, grain could be stored in granaries[19] for the winters; which were slightly colder than those of today. This was very much a communal lifestyle.[20]

Near to Stonehenge, the town of Durrington was vast by neolithic standards: It covered 17 hectares (42 acres) and was filled with rows of small square houses about 5 metres (16') wide.[21] Much of the activity in this town appears to have taken place over a very short period, leading archaeologists to think that construction may have lasted only decades rather than centuries.[22]

At this town, red deer antlers were used for digging and construction on "a truly grand scale":[23] At least 400 discarded antler picks have been discovered. This work began between 2525-2470 BC and ended sometime between 2480-2440 BC.[24] But radio carbon dates show that the town continued to be in use for quite a while longer.[22]

To the east, the River Avon flowed much deeper and wider than today,[25] providing a ready source of water for the town. It is possible that river craft also sailed these waters: Rope, made from honeysuckle or the stripped bark of the lime tree, would have been readily available and longboats & frail coracle-like craft had been around for some 3000 years.

The archaeologist and writer Francis Pryor has noted that *"Britain is alone in Northern and Atlantic Europe in having produced several examples of Earlier Bronze age plank built boats".*[26] Even at the earliest stages, Britain appears to have been a sea-faring nation.

In some ways the people of the area were different. Some Wessex skulls have been found to be quite child-like: Men may have been quite similar in appearance to women and their facial features refined and dainty. With noses, for instance, small and turned up,[27] these people were young and of a slight and slender build.[28]

But near Stonehenge, they were not relying solely on stored grain to survive. Instead, the people were feasting in mid-winter (and also possibly mid-summer[29]) on young roasted and stewed pork[30] brought here from all over the country.[31] We know of the winter timing because the pig teeth came from domestic animals born in the spring; nine months before the winter slaughter.[32]

This was a party. It was a big party and it was filled with young men and women. Whatever was going on, it became so well known that people from all over Europe started to come.

The path to Stonehenge

Though we know little of the lowland tracks, at high level it is easier to see where you are going, so these routes probably formed the easiest method of early travel and discovery. The Great Ridgeway, (also known as the Icknield Way), is an ancient track-way which runs from Norfolk across the Chilterns to Avebury, where it joins with a track-way from the Cotswolds before turning down towards, and then around, Stonehenge. Another track-way, the Harrow or 'Old Way' (and now sometimes known as the Pilgrim's Way), runs from the farthest point of Kent across the North Downs to Stonehenge.

The Harrow way is noted in old texts as having a branch which runs up to Avebury and down to Winchester.[41] The main route continues on, along or parallel to what is now the A303, and eventually meets up with the Great Ridgeway before running down to Dorset. In this vicinity, many other tracks meet and lead down to Old Sarum (Salisbury), the West and its tin mining country.

Composite map of routes
Map compiled from various references: (See notes: 42-44)

1: AN INTRODUCTION TO STONEHENGE

The South Downs track-way, known to be some eight thousand years old,[45] runs upwards from Eastbourne alongside a dense network of neolithic earthworks close to Combe Hill.[46] It then turns westwards through areas only fully cleared of trees in the later Bronze Age.[47] From here, it continues along the high ridges of the South Downs before turning north at Butser Hill (in Hampshire) to continue on to Winchester. Beyond Winchester, it joins other track-ways from the west of England, where some paths are known to be the oldest man-made roads in Europe.[48]

From Christchurch, on the south coast and directly south of Stonehenge, another track[49] leads to the same path-way network and then continues on towards Stonehenge. The map shown above is a compilation of probable main routes which have been compiled from various sources.[42-44] But no doubt there were many other tracks; far more than can be shown at this scale.

In the old visitor's car park, three pits, probably containing posts, have been dated to the period when these tracks were first used; some eight to nine thousand years ago.[50] Surrounding this point is an area of some 153 square kilometres, centred on Stonehenge, in which there are more than three hundred Scheduled Monuments of National Importance.[51] The largest settlement of its day in Northern Europe was built at Durrington; and this was followed by Stonehenge. Something very special was happening here, and it was happening long before the stones arrived.

Artistic impression of a Neolithic house

In the later Roman period, all roads would lead to Rome. But before the Romans came, all roads appear to have led to Stonehenge: Wherever you came from, getting to Stonehenge was simply a case of finding the track that everyone else was on.

Stonehenge: The word

It is thought that the word 'Stan' comes from the old English word for stone.[61] This is the simplest and most obvious suggestion: Many North European languages have a word for stone which sounds like the English word (examples are 'sten' and 'stein').

However, in Celtic languages from the Atlantic fringe, the word meaning 'stone' is quite different.[62] In Cornish, the word 'sten' means the metal tin. In Irish, 'stáin' also means tin and similar words for tin can be found in Catalan, Spanish and Latin. The word 'tin', with or without the 's', seems to be universal throughout Europe. Although the Roman Empire did not expand into all of these countries, this word may be derived from the Latin word 'Stannum'.

The word 'henge' is nowadays used in English to describe a circular structure, often a bank, ditch and/or mound sometimes accompanied by standing stones.[63] It was first used in 1932 by a British museum keeper, Thomas Kendrick, to describe a circular "sacred place".[64] Parts of all of these types of structure are found at Stonehenge, which thus gave the name 'henge' to all the other monuments: Nobody knew what 'henge' meant and it seemed as good a word as any. As time went by, the word 'henge' has been more strictly defined and, rather bizarrely, Stonehenge is no longer classified as a 'henge'.[65]

William Stuckely, an early historian of the monument, thought that the word henge was *"plainly Saxon & signifys only the hanging stones"*: Perhaps a form of stone gallows.[66] But though hangings were carried out at Stonehenge in the middle ages, there is no evidence that it was built to be a place of execution.

On the other hand, a 'hinge' is something that allows a door to swing open. 'Hænge', 'Hengsel', 'Hing', 'Hinge', 'Eŋge' and 'Gångjärn' are all words which mean hinge in North European languages. Similarly pronounced words for a 'hinge' exist in South European languages; for example 'Engoznar', 'Ganghero' & 'Engonçar'.

'Angel' can also mean hinge, pole or rod in other languages. Angleterre is the French word for England; Land of the Angles (a people of Saxon origin). Whatever language one uses in Europe, the word used to describe England is likely to sound like the word for hinge in that language.

1: AN INTRODUCTION TO STONEHENGE

Some European words with similar sounds:

	Hinge	*Rod (pole)*	*Angle*	*Tin*	*Stone*
Swedish:	gångjärn	stång	vinkel	tenn	sten
Irish	hinge	slat	uillinn	stáin	cloch
Cornish	---	---	---	sten	---
Scottish Gaelic	---	---	---	staoin	cloiche
Norwegian	hengsel	stang	vinkel	tinn	stein
Breton	---	---	angle	staen	(men)
Dutch	hengsel	stang	hengelen	tin	steen
German	angel	stange or angel	winkel	tin	stein
Faroese	hongsl	stong	vinkel	tin	steinur
Latvian	eņģe	stienis	leņķis	---	---
Danish	hængsel	stang	vinkel	tin	sten
Estonian	hing	---	vinkel	tina	---
Romanian	---	---	---	staniu	---
Latin	cardo	---	---	stannum	lapis
Welsh	dibynnu	gwialen	ongl	tun	---

--- word not found or word in that language not similar

Curiously, all these words seem to be related: It is almost as if the words Stone and Henge are deeply embedded in European languages; and meaning something to do with hinges, poles, angles, tin and stone.

A history of discovery

Stonehenge was first mentioned in a deed of 937 AD,[01] though few people have ever been certain what purpose the stones served. The diarist Samuel Pepys wrote *"God knows what their use was"*[02] whilst Daniel Defoe defeatedly recorded that *"all that can be learn'd from them is, that here they are"*.[03]

Though no Roman historian mentions the monument,[04] in the Historia Anglorum of 1129-30 AD, Henry of Huntingdon wrote of *'Stanenges'*, the *'second wonder of Britain'*,[05] that *"no-one can conceive how such great stones have been raised aloft, or why they were built here"*.[06]

In about 1620, King James the First requested the architect Indigo Jones to record the stones and find out their mysteries. Jones became convinced that it was a Roman temple and that one extra trilithon had once existed:

Illustration by Indigo Jones[07]

At the instigation of King Charles the Second, John Aubrey started his survey, largely due to a Court argument about whether it was a Roman temple or a coronation place of Danish kings.[08] Aubrey discovered both that Indigo Jones' survey was not very accurate and that a ring of mysterious holes had once existed:[09] Fifty six of these holes are located at the perimeter and are known as the 'Aubrey holes'.

Following Aubrey, William Stuckeley, a friend of both Edmund Halley and Issac Newton, re-surveyed the stones and realised that they were aligned to the sun's position along the horizon at solstice. Stuckeley was the first to suggest that Stonehenge dated prior to the birth of Christ and that it was a Druidic Temple.[10] He also discovered two cursuses near Stonehenge: Wide and very long areas, with banks of chalk either side, which were later found to have been built much earlier than the stones.

John Wood, an architect, also surveyed the monument at about the same time and vehemently disagreed with Stuckeley; thinking it to be a 'Druidic University' filled with Greek scholars.[11]

In 1877, Flinders Petrie allocated a number sequence to the stones, which is still in use today:[12] His system was to start at the north east entrance and to number the stones clockwise. Charles Darwin, who visited the site in 1888,[13] also pitched in and suggested that earthworms had played a major part in the submergence of some of the stones. By now, the gentry of England had acquired a fascination for Stonehenge.

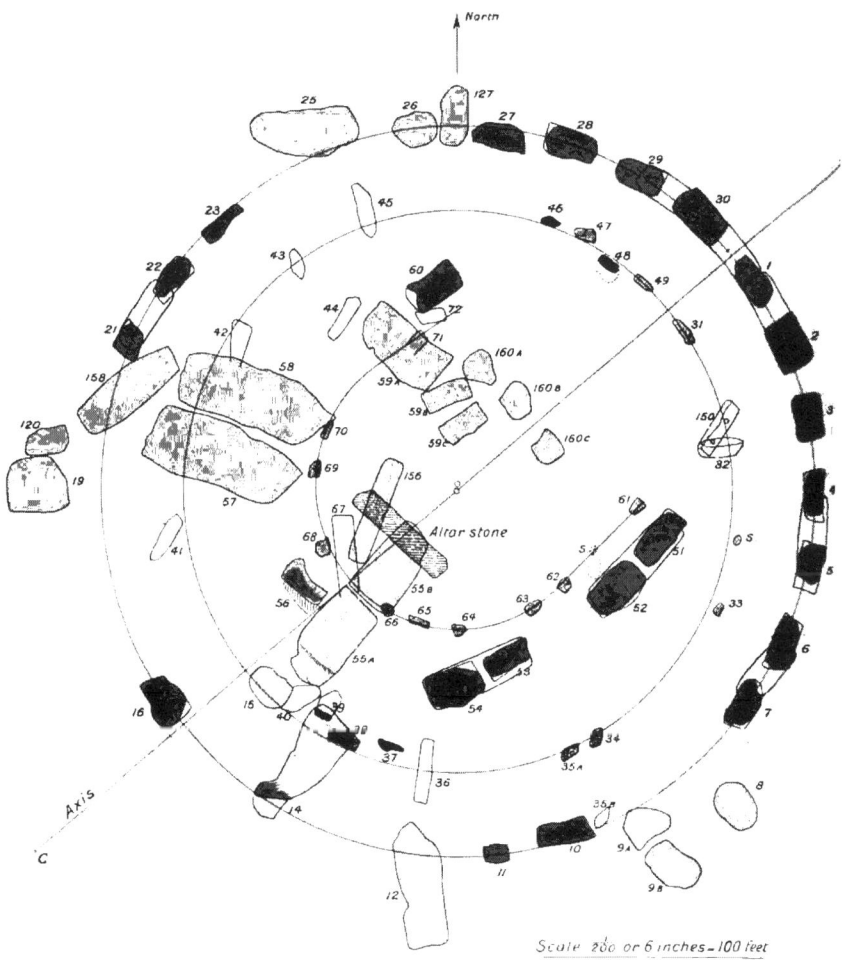

Barclay's plan of 1895 (Plan I) [14]

In 1900, one of the sarsen stones of the outer circle, together with its lintel, fell over. With growing concern, plans for restoration works were immediately put into place. Professor Gowland's straightening of the Great Trilithon [15] was undertaken the next year followed by several other restorations in the following decades. In Gowland's opinion, Stonehenge was *"a place of sanctity dedicated to the observation or adoration of the sun"*. [16]

Barclay's vision of Stonehenge when restored (1895) [17]

At the end of the Great War, in 1919, a certain Colonel Hawley was charged with excavated an extensive area of the site. It would not be unfair to say that modern archaeologists are not very impressed with the colonel's methods: A lot of information appears to have been mislaid and his finds are not always well recorded. Half a decade was to pass before the archaeologist Richard Atkinson became the last person to excavate large parts of the site. Even today, only about half of Stonehenge has ever been excavated. [18]

In 1995, the excellent volume 'Stonehenge in its Landscape' was published, bringing together all the information available at that time. However, this is a large technical volume and not for the faint-hearted. More recently, a vast amount of research and excavation in the neighbourhood of Stonehenge, together with some non destructive work at Stonehenge using new scanning technology, has been done by the Stonehenge Riverside Project.

But the one thing that pushed Stonehenge even further into the limelight was Gerald Hawkins' suggestion that the fifty-six Aubrey holes had been used both to predict movement of the moon and to predict eclipses of the sun.[19] Astronomers such as Fred Hoyle and John North followed later with even more detailed work.

Hoyle wrote: *"Nobody, as far as I am aware, has argued that the axis of Stonehenge is only accidentally coincident with the direction of midsummer sunrise".* [20] As proof, Hoyle noted that Sarmizegetusa, a superficially similar prehistoric monument near the village of Grădiste in Romania, is also aligned to a solstice horizon event, though the opposite time of day to the one at Stonehenge.[21]

However, whilst Sarmizegetusa may be aligned, no solstitial alignments have been found locally at any of the other great 'henges' of Wessex.[22] More recently still, Professor Clive Ruggles reviewed all these claims and concluded that only a few of the 'Stonehenge alignments' can be explained satisfactorily. Clive's view seems to be that Stonehenge was not an observatory.[23] In the last few years, Anthony Johnson reviewed Stonehenge's symmetry and concluded: *"My own opinion is that Stonehenge has only one alignment, i.e. the major line of symmetry established along the line of the summer-winter solstices".* [24]

From the excavations in the Avenue, it is thought that stones may have existed long before Stonehenge was erected. And some form of early 'solstice alignment' is now thought to have been in place centuries before the stones of Stonehenge were put up.

So a puzzle that remains is whether or not Stonehenge, the place that we know now, was purposefully aligned to solstice. If it was, what purpose was served by building such a large monument in a position which blocks the view in both directions?

A potted history of the monument's phases

In about 2500 BC, a massive forty two acre town was being built close to Stonehenge. This was to become the largest settlement of its day in Northern Europe.[31] It is thought that the people of this town, now known as Durrington, also built Stonehenge.[32]

About five thousand years before, a tree and three high posts, in a line some 37m (120') long, were put up some 250m (820') north west of Stonehenge. This can be found within what used to be the old car park,[33] and marks the beginning of whatever Stonehenge stood for. These posts were up to 70cm (≈2¼') in diameter[34] and made of pine; probably selected from the local pine and hazel woodland of that early period.

These posts are now dated to some ten thousand years ago, with only one exception (post hole 'B') having a later carbon-date.[35] However, a tree can be several hundred years old and, if one sample is taken from the old part of a tree and another from the young part, carbon dating will show different dates.[36]

Professor Timothy Darvill uses the phrase *"Tamed Wildwood"* to describe the landscape of the following period (from about 4000 to 3000 BC.)[37] Pine had given way to a mixture of elm, ash, oak, hazel and yew[38] with large felled areas of open grassland and some localised farming. At about this time, the Lesser Cursus, and the Great Cursus, were built towards the north west and the north of Stonehenge.[39]

This was a period in which cursuses had become fashionable[40] throughout the British Isles, though not on the continent.[41] The earliest cursuses are in Scotland and generally fall within the date range of 3660-3370 BC.[42] One curious feature of cursuses is that they do not generally *seem* to align to anything.

1: AN INTRODUCTION TO STONEHENGE

In the same period, leading up to 3000 BC, other monuments are known to be exactly aligned to solstice; for instance Newgrange in Ireland.[43] From our knowledge of Newgrange, other alignments such as those of Knowth (to equinox) have been assumed or deduced.[44] But these are rarely an exact match: A few early cursuses point in the general direction of a solstice event, but of more than a hundred or so other cursuses and passage tombs in Britain, very few have obvious alignments.[45]

The timing of the construction of the various stages at Stonehenge was most recently revised in 'The Age of Stonehenge'.[46] These new dates have significantly modified what was previously thought to have been the construction sequence.

Dates are arrived at by using the decay rate of carbon-14 (C-14); an unstable, but relatively long lived, hybrid of carbon-12 which is formed in the upper atmosphere. As the sun's cosmic rays cause atoms to be broken, a small portion of the broken atomic parts join together, more or less at random, to form carbon-14.[47] The atoms of C-14 then join with others to form molecules which gradually disperse down into the lower atmosphere, where they are converted by plants using sunlight (a process known as photosynthesis).

At the time the plant dies, it stops taking in C-14; which then gradually decays into nitrogen. By working out how much C-14 is left in a plant, or an animal which eats those plants, the age of the sample can be estimated. The way this is done is reasonably accurate and relies on knowing how much solar activity occurred in the past. However, the method is only statistical and can be subject to quite a lot of error.

As the fourth millennium BC ended, a new era of continental weather conditions arrived: Drier and warmer summers with colder winters.[48] By 3000 BC, the area around Stonehenge contained a lightly wooded and open grassy plain, not dissimilar to that which we can see today.[49]

At about the same time, something else was going on at Stonehenge: A large number of post-holes were being dug at its centre. Although much of the ground has not been excavated, over two hundred holes are known to exist.[50] The date that these holes were dug is not known, but a well known expert, Professor Stuart Piggott, thought there may have been a timber central structure on the site.

But prior to this, a series of periglacial stripes (natural geological features), are currently thought to have existed: Some of which seem to align to sunset at solstice.[51] Whatever happened to cause the solstice alignment to eventually be settled upon, it is possible that it was, like Newgrange, a key feature of the early stages.

Newgrange: Ireland

At that particular moment in time, some other similarities with the solstice-aligned Newgrange are also evident: In the Newgrange complex, there is another major monument called Knowth. This monument has two passages which both look towards the horizon: Both passages are slightly off-set from equinox; and one slightly more than the other. The passage nearer to the equinox 'alignment' is the longer of the two.

Before the major building work took place, Stonehenge, like Newgrange, probably had an 'alignment' which pointed towards a solstice. Stonehenge's cursuses also both look towards the horizon. Like Knowth, both cursuses are slightly off-set from equinox. And one, the Lesser Cursus, is off-set slightly more than the other. In addition, the Greater Cursus, nearer to the equinox 'alignment', is the longer of the two.

Newgrange seen from Knowth, Ireland

Potted history: Stage 1 *(3000-2920 BC)*

The first major building phase included a circular embankment, which could have been up to two metres (6') high, and was built to surround the central area. The bank stands on a base 6m (20') wide and has a diameter of almost 100m (≈300').[61] Outside the bank there is a ditch and a small second bank of chalk beyond (known as the counter-scarp), which could have been up to 75cm (2½') high.[62] The ditch between the two is the easiest to date using carbon-14 because of the antler pick-axes left behind by the workers.[63]

Below the bank there exist post-holes of some 20cm (8") diameter and 50cm (20") apart, possibly indicating an earlier phase.[64] There were two entrances through this bank: One main entry at the north east, some 12m (40') wide,[65] and a smaller 3.5m (≈12') entry to the south.[66] This second entry is a few degrees off direct south. It is also possible that a third entrance existed to the south west.

At this stage, periglacial stripes may have been visible along the 'solstice alignment'. It is also possible that one or more stones existed in a line; very slightly off-centre relative to a 'solstice line'. A series of timber posts are also known to have existed, more or less in line with the centre of the entrance: These posts were roughly in the position of the moon's alignment at its furthest position on the horizon.

Artistic view of the early henge along the 'solstice alignment'

Within the inner bank, the Aubrey holes were dug[67] around about 3000 BC.[68] If these holes held posts, they may have been up to 10m (≈30') high. There were fifty-six of these holes; dug in a near perfect circle and very accurately set out. These were cut some 0.56m (22") to 1.14m (45") down, with the deeper holes at the higher ground suggesting that the level of whatever went into those holes may have been important.[69]

The Aubrey holes vary between 0.74m (30") and 1.82m (72") diameter,[70] but show no alignment to the skies. Like the southern entrance, they are two or three degrees out from cardinal directions (north, south, east, west). Though the Aubreys may have been important, the amount of effort required to construct the circular embankment would have far exceeded the effort required to dig these holes.

The main entrance originally aligned several degrees north of solstice, but was at some point relocated so that it looked to the same general direction as the Avenue.[71] Along what later became that Avenue, one or more stones already existed, or where perhaps installed at a later intermediate date, in what appears to be the solstice alignment.

At this time, the cursuses and their banks would still have been the major feature of the area. These were, and still are, huge compared to Stonehenge's circular bank.

Artistic impression: The Great Cursus and Stonehenge seen to scale from above

Chalk plaques, with zig-zag patterns similar in some ways to those found on stones at Newgrange and Knowth, have since been discovered in the area. These have been dated to a similar period to that in which the bank and holes were constructed (2900-2590 BC).[72]

Potted History: Stage 2 *(2620-2480 BC)*

The five huge stone trilithons in the centre of Stonehenge were most likely the next major element. This was probably followed by a double arc arrangement known as the Q and R holes. These holes probably consisted of a ring together with an internal arc at the north east.[81]

26m (85') and 22.5m (74') diameter respectively, this ring and arc probably contained bluestones.[82] Each may have been topped with a lintel,[83] possibly to make an early version of Stonehenge (the bases of these holes have been found to contain dolerite chips).

If it was intended to eventually have two full rings, there would have been forty pairs of stones, together with a possible third partial mini-arc set inside these stones. It is not known whether or not these were abandoned before completion as excavation has only been carried out in the eastern and western quarters.[84]

At this stage, whatever was being constructed did not fully reflect either the alignment nor the symmetry of what would come later. Other than the trilithons, as it now seems likely that they were erected in this early stage, this arrangement seems to have first pointed towards the centre of the old entrance. It also seems probable that the sarsen circle we know today was erected some time after the trilithons.

Whilst likely, it is also not known whether the Q and R stones were immediately removed; this process may have occurred over a period of one or more hundred years.

The Heel-stone, some D-shaped buildings and the Station Stones were also probably put in place during this phase. Beyond the north east entrance, the Heel-stone may have been moved from stone hole 97 (in the old line of stone holes) to its new position. As Mike Pitts recalls: *"we know (from my own excavation) that a megalith used to stand beside the Heelstone, and that after this was erected, and probably after it had been taken away, the Heelstone was surrounded by a small circular ditch"*.[85]

Stone hole 97 is substantial, 1.75m (5'9") across[86] and 1m (≈3') deep. Whatever existed there had been part of a row which roughly pointed towards solstice, but could also have pointed to a major moon stand-still.

For reasons that are not known, this alignment (along what would become the Avenue) was removed. The only major stone along this line (the Heel-stone) was probably relocated to a new position in which it has remained to this day. As the archaeologist Aubrey Burl (quoting Neil) explains: *"It is always assumed that it was from the centre of the sarsen circle that the observations were made, but, from that position, as pointed out in 1975, 'the sun ought to rise to the right at the top of the heelstone on the morning of 21 June our time. But it does not; it rises about a foot and a half to the left'"*.[87]

The Heel-stone's new position as seen from along the centre-line

Many people have suggested that the name of the Heel-stone was derived from the Greek word for the sun: 'Helios'. If it was, it is very curious that the builders would choose to move it so that it did not align with the sun. Interestingly, the English word wheel comes from the Old English word hwēol, which derives from the meaning 'to revolve, move around'.

Potted history: Stage 3 *(2480-2280 BC)*

In the third stage, the Avenue was built (or, perhaps improved), the ditch cleaned and mounds raised to form the north and south barrows around two of the Station Stones. The Slaughter-stone companions, (in stone holes D and E) were probably erected in the previous phase, but were probably now taken down, to widen the north east entrance. A large pit was also dug into north side of Great Trilithon.[88]

However, whilst the Avenue had bluestone and sarsen chippings beneath its banks[89]; indicating that it was built up in this later phase, it is not certain that some form of Avenue had not existed earlier.

The Avenue: Barclay's extract from Stuckeley (1895)[90]

It was thought that the Avenue had once been constructed in two phases. However, in his recent book, Professor Parker Pearson describes how no evidence of this has been found:[91]

> "The stretch of avenue in which we were most interested was where the magnetometer survey had shown a kink in the ditches, suggesting that a new stretch of avenue had possibly been tacked on to the end of the 500-metre-long straight section. In reality, we could see on the ground that there was no such deviation: the bend joined seamlessly with the straight section."

In addition, the Avenue bend was not rutted, leading to the conclusion that it was unlikely to have been used for processions.[92]

Potted history: Stage 4 & 5 (*2280-2020 BC and 1680-1520 BC*)

The Q and R stones were rearranged into the outer bluestone circle (between 2270 and 2020 BC) and a bluestone oval set within the trilithons (2210-1930 BC). The inner bluestone 'horse-shoe' may be all that remains of the oval and its stones, repositioned from the earlier Q and R ring.[93]

Nearly a thousand years after the stones were first erected, two circles of rectangular holes, known as the Y and Z circles, were constructed in about 1640-1520 BC.[94] Located just outside the sarsen outer ring, there is no evidence that these holes, apparently separated by a period of between one or more hundred years, ever held stones.[95]

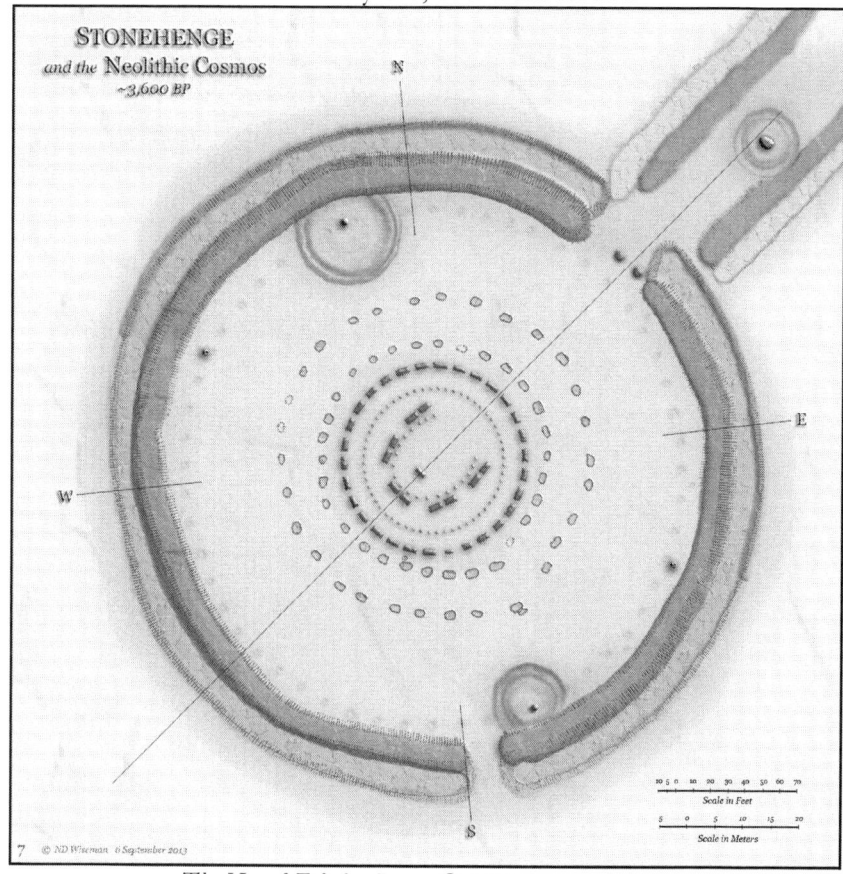

The Y and Z holes. Image © ND Wiseman 2013

The Stones: A potted summary

Stonehenge contains well over one thousand tons of Stone.[01] The majority of this is sarsen; a fine grained type of siliceous sandstone[02] formed under extreme pressure. Grains of quartz sand become bound together with siliceous cement[03] to form a stone which is harder than granite. In 1654, the diarist John Evelyn wrote of this material: *"The Stone is so exceedingly hard, that all my strength with a hammer could not break a fragment".*[04]

The smaller bluestones, on the other hand, are a much softer material. The glaciers of the last Ice Age never got as far as the Salisbury Plain,[05] so the bluestones are generally thought to have been hauled from the Mynydd Preseli area of Wales[06] by gangs of workers.

Geoffrey of Monmouth, in his 'History of the Kings of Britain',[07] wrote that the Stonehenge Circle was originally erected in Ireland from stones brought from Africa. However, it is much more likely that the larger sarsen stones were brought from the nearby Marlborough Plain. This area is some twenty miles to the north, near the larger (and earlier) sarsen monument of Avebury.

The outer perimeter of Avebury today

The sarsens were probably buried below ground[08] and specifically sought out by the Stonehenge builders. Given that Avebury already existed, and that there is lots of sarsen stone available in that area, this type of stone would have been well known. How these stones were transported, over almost twenty miles of uneven countryside,[09] remains a mystery.

Stonehenge is one of the only monuments in Britain where megaliths were carved. It is likely that these were made by flaking the natural blocks to get a rough shape[10] and then chipping away at the surface using mauls[11] weighing up to 26 kilograms.[12] The distribution of flakes shows that the bluestones were dressed inside the circle, whereas the sarsens were worked outside the ditch and bank.[13]

At the perimeter of the main stone circle, there once existed up to thirty of these massive uprights; not all equal in size but placed with their centres at almost exactly the same distance.[15] Typically weighing 25 tons, these uprights average some 4.1m (13½') high[16] and are topped with lintels weighing up to 6 tons.

There was an obvious intent to make the circle perfect: Some uprights are longer than others and were buried to the depth needed to make an exactly level top-most ring.[14] After the stones were erected, the shaped lintels were then raised into position.

The smoother faces of the sarsen circle uprights look inwards and are set on a true circle of just under 30m (≈100') in diameter.[17] First noted by Stuckeley, these sarsens are worked more finely and smoothly on the inside[18] and, to a small extent, dressed to be gently tapering upwards (an architectural device known as entasis). This effect might have been used to help create the optical illusion of straightness.[19]

Stones of the outer circle drawn from slightly off-centre

Dovetailed and attached with mortice and tenon joints, the stones which were to become lintels were also finely worked on the inner faces and then placed to be precisely level on the top surface.[20] Whilst not quite as good as we can achieve today, the accuracy to which this monument was set out is quite astonishing.

Within the middle of the monument, five sets of paired upright stones exist onto which even more massive lintels were lifted. These sets are known as 'trilithons' and are arranged symmetrically about the single largest stone set; known as the Great Trilithon. The largest of the uprights weighs in excess of 40 tons, and each was carefully worked, with considerable effort, to make one face as smooth as possible. With only one exception, these smooth faces look inwards:[21] The Great Trilithon is unique in having its smoother, flatter face look out rather than in.[22]

Atop of the trilithon uprights, the lintels are about 1m ($\approx$40") deep and 1.2m ($\approx$47") wide; except for the Great Trilithon lintel which is only 70cm (27") deep. The tops of lintels are 6m ($\approx$20'), 6.25m ($\approx$21') and 7.5m ($\approx$25') above ground[23] and, in all cases, the lintels have been shaped and then fitted onto the uprights with mortise and tenon joints formed in stone.[24]

A lintel of one of the trilithons

The Great Trilithon was tilted back to position at the start of the last century, with the result that its new position is slightly rotated and also further away from the centre of the monument; by as much as 60cm[25] ($\approx$24") from its original location.[26] A huge pit was later extended from the Great Trilithon and, allowing for this, these trilithons have been dated to 2620-2480 BC.[27]

The sarsen stones of the monument are largely symmetrical with but two curious exceptions: Firstly, a smaller than usual stone exists in the outer circle and directly south of centre; perhaps making a larger than usual opening. One of the Trilithon pairs also stands out as being unique:

Stone 54 stands directly south of the centre and has a 'foot' about twice the width of the rest of this stone.[28] Despite being shorter than the Great Trilithon, it is the heaviest stone. This upright was also constructed in a unique fashion: It was packed with a hard compact rock which *"cannot, as yet, be referred to any of the existing stones, was used as packing for stone 54".*[29]

Set just inside the outer sarsen circle, a smaller ring of stones known as the 'bluestone circle' are arranged with a diameter of 23-24m (75'-79').[30] These stones are variable in size and shape; some 2m (6'6") or higher above ground[31] with a spacing of about 2.7m (9').[32]

Most of the stones in this circle show little sign of having been dressed.[33] However, Stone 36 was found partially buried and this stone does show indications of having been a lintel: It was beautifully worked and the mortice holes are too close to centre to be a lintel ring.[34] If it was a lintel, this stone would have been part of an early 'trilithon configuration'.

Within the sarsen horse-shoe, another set of smaller blue stones, up to 2.5m (8') high and spaced 3.5m (11½') apart,[35] were arranged as an oval and graded in height: The shortest stones occur at the horse-shoe edge and the highest were towards the back (near the Great Trilithon).[36]

Originally, this was almost certainly an oval shape, which was modified at later date.[37] It contained the most finely worked of the bluestones.[38] At least two abandoned arrangements, from the remains of earlier oval patterns, were found in front of the horse-shoe.[39]

Bluestones within the inner monument

The axis of the monument

Where architects can, they will design buildings to be symmetrical: Symmetry is more pleasing to the eye. Even a standard English semi-detached house will almost always be symmetrical about the division wall between the two properties.

Stonehenge too is a largely symmetrical monument and, from its symmetry, the axis has been established (it now appears that the Avenue was built long after the monument). However, there are a few exceptions to the symmetry of this stone monument. Perhaps clues to its meaning can be found from looking at what does not fit this symmetrical pattern.

Long before the stones were erected, the main opening through the great henge's bank wall pointed more towards the north: A series of posts holes, probably timber, existed at and outside the entry [01] (anti-clockwise of the eventual stone alignment). At some point, the bearing was shifted to 49.9° from north (originally 46.55°) [02] and a series of stone holes known as the C, B and 97 probably came to signify the choice of the final symmetry about the monument axis. [03] At this stage, stone hole 97 may have held the Heel-stone (now located in stone hole 96.) [04]

The Slaughter-stone, which fell over in centuries past, stood upright [05] some 5m (16') above the ground. This stone is estimated to weigh 28 tons and is located at the edge of the entry to the 100m (330') diameter henge. [06] Unlike many of the other out-lying stones, the Slaughter-stone was made to shape. [07] Two further holes, known as D and E, are some 4m (13') apart and, together with the Slaughter-stone, may once have symmetrically framed the entry. [08]

The fallen Slaughter-stone

However, stone hole 96, the eventual location of the Heel-stone, is an exception to the rule of symmetry. It cannot be established that 97 and the Heel-stone (86) were a pair[09] and, in fact, it looks very unlikely that they were: A ditch,[10] which cuts through the hole for 97, was later dug around the Heel-stone showing that the two holes were not of the same era. Stone hole 97 is 5m (≈16') long and might have held a sarsen which was then moved to the Heel-stone position; and only later had a ditch constructed around it.[11]

A heel is the point of the foot about which you rotate: It gives rise to the English phrase 'turn on one's heel'; meaning to make a sudden change of direction. Over four thousand years ago, something curious happened at the location of the Heel-stone: Its alignment was changed, and specifically modified, so that it no longer aligned with the rest of the stone structure.

The four Station Stones, located in the same boundary circle formed by the earlier Aubrey holes, are arranged as an almost exact parallelogram about 80m (262') by 33.5m (110') wide.[12] Only stones 91 and 93 survive, but the two missing stones (92 and 94) had low chalk mounds around them; together with encircling ditches. These were originally thought to be for burial, so are still known as the north and south barrows.[13]

These Station Stones, or the remains of their holes, are said to be approximately aligned on the most southerly moon-rise and most northerly moon-set.[14] However, at this latitude, any box will align to these lunar events if one edge of the box points towards a solstice horizon event (sunrise or sunset).

A further suggestion was that the diagonal between stones had some sort of astronomical significance; thus explaining why they were not arranged in the shape of a square or a line. However, the astronomer Clive Ruggles notes:

"The question of why the station stones were placed in a rectangle and not a square has given rise in the past to the tentative suggestion that the WNW-ESE diagonal might have had astronomical significance; however its declination -16°, has no obvious explanation in terms of the Sun or Moon and in any case the diagonal passes across the centre of the site where it might have been partially obscured by the bluestones, and certainly would have been obscured by the later sarsens". [15]

Metals & Stonehenge

Between 6000 and 7000 BC, copper was being hammered at Çatal Hüyük in Turkey.[08] The earliest mirrors, made of polished obsidian, have also been found at Çatal Hüyük and dated to about 6200 BC.[09] The earliest copper mirrors found so far date to about 4000 BC.

Professor Gowland, whilst re-erecting Stone 56 (part of the Great Trilithon), found traces of copper carbonate some seven feet (≈2m) down.[01] This relic of a long lost object indicates that copper was being used whilst the holes were being dug.
    Two chalk blocks discovered by Mike Parker Pearson at Durrington have long thin V cuts showing the probable use of a metal axe. The ditch in which these were found dates to 2480-2460 BC. Beaker copper composition also hints at a date one or two centuries earlier than 2400BC. In addition, the change in the size of trees felled around Stonehenge shows that metals technology had been introduced prior to its construction.[02] By 2500 BC, metal technology found in and around the Stonehenge barrows also shows that extensive trading networks had become established within the region.[03]
    In 1586, a tin plaque was found at Stonehenge and noted by the traveller William Camden. Stuckeley was later to say: *"But eternally to be lamented is the loss of that tablet of tin, which was found at this place... inscirb'd with many letters... No doubt it was a memorial of the founders, wrote by the Druids, and had it been preserv'd till now, would have been an invaluable curiosity."*[04]

The evidence that metals were being used before Stonehenge was built is therefore quite extensive. Copper and tin came from localities 200-300km to the west[05] and, as a result of Parker Pearson's findings, the Copper Age is now known to date back to 2500-2200 BC.[06]
    In the book; 'The Early British Tin Industry', its author Gerrard notes that: *"Detailed electron probe micro-analysis of European Bronzes has led Professor Northover to suggest that "the number of metal sources used at one time was very limited, and there was often only one". Consequently, trading of metals was on a large scale and this phenomenon he termed the "metal circulation zone". For the Early Bronze Age, Northover has noted that tin bronzes were probably exclusively produced in Britain from South Western cassiterite."*[07]
    In other words, all early tin throughout Europe probably came from one place. That one place was probably Cornwall.

Professor Parker Pearson describes how metals are now thought to have been in use at the time Stonehenge was constructed:

> "We can date the ditch-digging to 2480-2460 BC so have a clue that someone was using a copper axe slightly earlier than expected."
>
> "Another tell-tale is the change in tree-felling after about 2500BC.... After this date, we find monuments built of timbers up to about a metre in diameter....Perhaps what was special about that moment around 2500 BC was that copper axes became available in sufficient numbers in Britain to fell much larger trees with greater ease."

In the book 'Tin in Antiquity', Roger Penhallurick describes[10] how a large piece of timber, worked by hand tools, was found in 1839 during the mining of a deep bed of tin ore (cassiterite) in Cornwall. Too young to have been deposited by nature, carbon dating showed that it was as old, or much older, than Stonehenge. Below is the full extract of description, produced for The Institute of Metals:

> "Sub-fossil wood resting on top of the tin ground ought to have a date of c. 10000 bp, or even earlier. Wood found within the tin ground cannot have arrived there at the same time as the cassiterite, and it can hardly be doubted that Winn's oak trunk had been put there by man. It has been dated at the University of California, Riverside (UCR 1828), to 4140 +/- 100 bp, giving a time range of 3015-2415 BC. This is uncomfortably early, even if the precise calendar date lies at the end of the range. It suggests that tin streaming in Cornwall began much earlier than hitherto suspected."

In other words, tin ore was almost certainly being mined long before Stonehenge was constructed.

New Evidence

In June 2012, Professor Parker Pearson and The Stonehenge Riverside Project published 'Stonehenge: Exploring the Greatest Stone Age Mystery.' This book summarises the results of seven years of exploration at the enigmatic timber and earthen monuments which surround Stonehenge.

In late 2012, English Heritage published an archaeological report entitled 'Stonehenge Laser Scan: Archaeological Investigation Report'; which contains many newly discovered details. Both of these publications contain fascinating new information about the lives of, and the monuments built by, the people who constructed Stonehenge.

Curiously, the latest scans have shown that there are over 100 images of a T shape carved into the faces of the stones at Stonehenge:

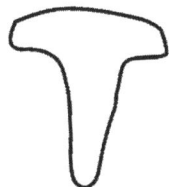

An example of the type of engraving found at Stonehenge

This type of engraving, thought to be an axe-head, does not occur to any extent anywhere else in the British Isles. The new report shows the 'axe-heads' to be concentrated on and around Stones 4, 5 and Stone 53. These stones reflect more non-symmetrical features of Stonehenge: Stone 53 is directly south of the centre and the other two stones are directly east.

Pages 28 to 31 of the report show that the majority of newly discovered markings exist on Stone 4, *the eastern stone*, with other 'T' shape markings existing on stones 3 and 5, either side of the eastern stone. Apart from these stones, few other engravings exist. Page 34 of the report shows that the majority of the other newly discovered 'T' shaped markings are on Stone 53.

Large 'T' shapes have also been discovered on the western side face of Stone 54, the eastern side face of stone 53 and the rear of both 53 & 54:

View of Stone 54 showing the 'T' shape
Photograph courtesy of Terence Meaden ©2013

It is almost as if the 'T' shape was particularly important at Stonehenge and, specifically, that it was especially important to stones 53 and 54.

The latest archaeological report[01] also shows more non-symmetry at the south point of the horse-shoe: Stone 54, the southern-most stone of the inner monument, is both the heaviest stone and the most notably unusual in comparison to others nearby:[02]

> "Though it is notable how well Stones 53 and 154 are finished in relation to Stone 54"

The report also states that the stones had been shaped to provide a view from the Avenue (in the north east):[03,04]

> "The most regular and extensively dressed stones are however placed towards the NE"

> "This confirms the view that the sarsen circle was not supposed to be approached, or perhaps even seen, from this southwest direction (Tilley et al. 2007). Instead the emphasis was on the approach from the NE"

And that stones had been designed *not* to be viewed from other angles. It states that the surface finish of the stones becomes progressively less good towards the south west:[05-07]

> "The use of small stones (e.g Stone 11 and Stone 21) and irregular stones (e.g. Stone 14) is a distinct feature of the SW half of the monument"

> "The absence of working on the exterior faces of Stones 14-16 and coarse finished on the backs of Stones 10 and 11 is significant as these further demonstrate a significant contrast between the NE and SW sides of the monument, as well as indicating interior/exterior differences"

> "The absence of dressing on the exterior surfaces of stones on the SW of the Sarsen Circle indicates that the monument was not designed to be approached from this direction"

The report also shows that the lintels to the north east are the most extensively worked:[08]

> "The lintels have been extensively shaped, with curved outer and inner faces matching the circumference of the monument"

> "Lintels 102 and 130, 101 and 102 on the NE half of the monument, are most regular lintels"

Theories

"The starting point is often not the body of archaeological evidence at all, but a theory which forms a mould into which all the disparate elements appear to fit". (Anthony Johnson.) [01]

As with the nearby monument of Avebury,[02] some scholars believe that Stonehenge was associated with death. Earlier theories include that it was a work of the Phonecians, a temple of the Druids, a monument of the British to Anaraith (a goddess), a monument to Queen Boadicea, a Roman temple, the burial place of Uther Pendragon and other kings or a Danish monument.[03] No doubt there were many other theories.

Noting the Druids' belief in reincarnation, and their known fascination with astronomy and the size of the world, Hancock[04] suggests the possibility that Stonehenge may have been connected to a spiritual quest for reincarnation and immortality of the soul. Terence Meaden suggests that Stonehenge was seen not just as a temple, but as a goddess in itself.[05]

Gerald Hawkins famously proposed that Stonehenge was a type of observatory of the stars.[06] However, Professor Hoyle, who advocated a similar position, remarked that *"When I first read Professor Hawkins' book Stonehenge Decoded, I was struck by the angular differences between the actual measured sight lines and the astronomical alignments"..* (shown by Prof Hawkins' book). *"Even with primitive equipment, a stone could still be placed to within about a foot".*[07] He also said that *"In one case in six, a purely arbitrary direction would happen by chance to agree with an astronomical alignment".* [08]

More strikingly, he notes that no account of the achievement has been made in *"the full light of documented history".*[09] This is perhaps key: If something spectacular happened at Stonehenge, there would be some sort of record, even if only in mythology.

Though the astronomical observatory theory is the most popular and well known, Professor Clive Ruggles has recently concluded that there is little, if any, evidence of intentional astronomical orientation in the early work,[10] nor evidence that the structures at Stonehenge *"deliberately incorporated a great many astronomical alignments, or that they served as any sort of computing device to predict eclipses."* [11]

1: AN INTRODUCTION TO STONEHENGE 33

The observatory theory seems to be dead as a result of Ruggles' work. This is not really a surprise given that Stonehenge's stones face inwards; and not in a direction that can be used for observation. Nevertheless, the earliest version of this monument did seem to point towards a 'solstice alignment'.

No theory has yet come to explain what Stonehenge was for. Some of the biggest mysteries are:

- What is the internally facing structure for?
- Why is it arranged with outlier stones and its huge bank?
- Why is there no record of what was done there?

As Johnson said in 2008: *"The starting point is often not the body of archaeological evidence at all, but a theory which forms a mould into which all the disparate elements appear to fit"*. The pages which follow will describe a new theory which will explain _all_ of the features described in the chapter you have just read.

2: STONEHENGE AND THE HINGE

The images in the following text were produced using a three dimensional computer model based on a similar newly invented renewable energy device. This was found to replicate the stones at Stonehenge as they may have been when first constructed. Stonehenge's plan layout is thus shown to be the same as an idealised geocentric description of the Universe.

Stonehenge was built at the dawning of a new age. In Egypt, the Pharaohs would soon start to build pyramids and in Britain, metals technology had just been introduced. A few hundred years later, tin and copper would be mixed to form bronze. With the discovery of alloys, the British Bronze Age would start and the Stone Age would become a thing of the past.

In this chapter, every feature of Stonehenge is shown to be explainable using a very old and little known way of scientific thinking combined with engineering principles. This introduction describes how the search for knowledge could have resulted in an early fundamental view of the Universe and the subsequent creation of Stonehenge itself.
  It has recently been discovered that metals were in use at the time Stonehenge was built. Metal has unique properties which, in addition to making good weapons, can be used in inventions. One such invention, a hinged mechanism which concentrates light, fits precisely into Stonehenge's structure. This light-concentrating system could be used to demonstrate how the Sun seems to move if the Earth is believed to be fixed at the centre of the Universe.

The times

At the time Stonehenge was built, it is believed that life revolved around herding, farming, hunting and gathering with some communities also producing pottery, wood-crafts and other skilled work such as the management of woodland for fuel and building. Mining, smelting and metalwork were newly discovered technologies.

Although science was in its infancy, the people of the time may have felt that they were undergoing the first industrial revolution.

Cornwall was a major source for tin ore (Cassiterite) and mines elsewhere could have produced copper and perhaps lead. But these new materials would have come at a very high cost: To make metal from ore, charcoal would have been made from a dried coppiced timber such as hazel. The ore has to be mined, smelted and then probably refined once again using a re-melting process. After smelting, metals are often re-worked again using heat.

All these processes are relatively dangerous work. At this time, metal objects would probably have taken more effort to produce than anything made of the old materials such as timber and stone: Shaping a large rock using a stone maul would be relatively easy compared to the effort and expertise required to make one saw. Whilst new technologies were being developed, storage of food would have remained critical to survival because prolonged winters could signal starvation for the community.

Long after Stonehenge, the Romans and Greeks believed that the world was at the centre of the Universe. Only recently have we come to accept that our world travels around the Sun. But on a world believed to be located at the centre, the Sun does not seem fixed at all; instead it appears to orbit the North Pole in summer before gradually moving to the south, where it spends the winter.

Today, a discovery mission has sent the rover, 'Curiosity', to the planet Mars. Similarly, our ancestors must have considered the whimsies of the Sun and Moon worthy of curiosity: These objects seem to move within the heavenly firmament, yet are seemingly not committed to a fixed position within it. If the Sun were thought capable of making slight changes to its own yearly cycle, the perception may have been that starvation could result from the Sun's action. If this were believed possible, inventions which could help to understand the heavens would be borne out of necessity, not curiosity.

Astronomy on a fixed world

Our world appears to be solid and fixed. If you were to be placed in a new computer generated Universe, somewhere which looks exactly like Southern England, there would be no obvious way to tell if you are on a disc, a ball, a cylinder or a flat endless plain. The Universe beyond our world might also be unknown: It could be a solid sphere, it could be stars with space between, or it could be something else entirely.

Simple experiments can help to show the nature of the world and the heavens. For example, the stars above us can be seen to move over the course of a night. A diligent observer, or someone with far too much time on their hands, will soon notice that some stars seem to move less than others.

By taking straight sticks and pointing them at those stars which appear to move the least, the polar axis of the world can be found: On returning a few hours later, the one stick which still points to the same unmoving star marks the most likely polar axis around which the rest of the stars rotate.

This experiment finds the fixed point of the heavens. The stick which was used to find it points along the apparent polar axis. At the time Stonehenge was built, this point was marked by a star called Thuban. But prior to Thuban there would have been no obvious marker for thousands of years.

Using the polar stick, another stick can be tied with string to make a sail which can be rotated like a hinge:

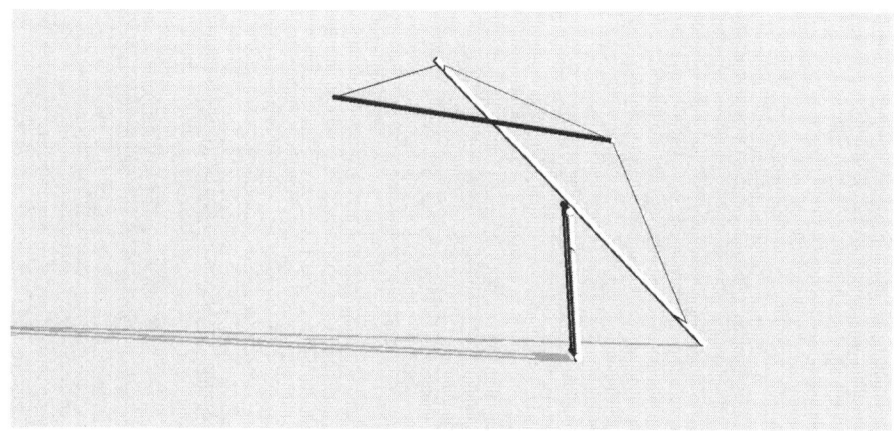

Tracing stars using the North Pole

2: STONEHENGE AND THE HINGE 37

Looking from the ground, this sail can be rotated to line up with other stars: As time goes by over the course of a summer night, the sail can be rotated slowly to keep pace with one star and other stars will then remain at the same point along the length of the sail. By counting, and moving the sail in small angular steps, it is possible to show that the skies work like a 24 hour clock.

The clock of the stars

This experiment shows that the Universe revolves. It does not show what shape the Universe has; a revolving ball would look much the same as a revolving cylinder, or even stars with space between them.

By looking down the length of the sail (rather than looking from the base of the polar stick), other stars can also be seen to be keeping pace. If the sail is at right angles to the pole, these stars will be near to the equatorial axis and are unique because they rise to the east and set to the west. The discovery of east and west stars can be very useful: By noting where equatorial stars set, from a location on high ground, the direction of something else (for instance a village) can found.

Following the stars

In the Northern Hemisphere, the best place to do this experiment is on a north facing slope. If the experiment is done in England over a long night of winter, the stars can be seen to rotate in almost a full circle. The most obvious explanation for this, if the Earth is fixed, is that the Universe is a sphere.

Even today, the most likely explanation for the Universe's shape is that it forms some sort of spheroid.

The sail of the stick can also be pointed towards the sun. Using exactly the same experiment, the sun can be shown to rotate around the same axis as the stars. In Southern England, at about 51° latitude, the sun can be seen to rotate around a stick which points up to the North Pole at about 51° from the ground. (Latitude, the number of degrees from the equator, can be found anywhere in the Northern Hemisphere by pointing a stick at the North Pole.)

During the spring and autumn equinoxes, a sail pointing to the sun will be at right-angles (perpendicular) to the pole-stick. To make it follow the sun in high summer, the stick must point up from perpendicular by about 24°. At winter equinox, around about the 21st of December, it must point down by about 24°. Like the stars, if the rotating stick is made to follow the sun, it also turns just like a 24 hour clock.

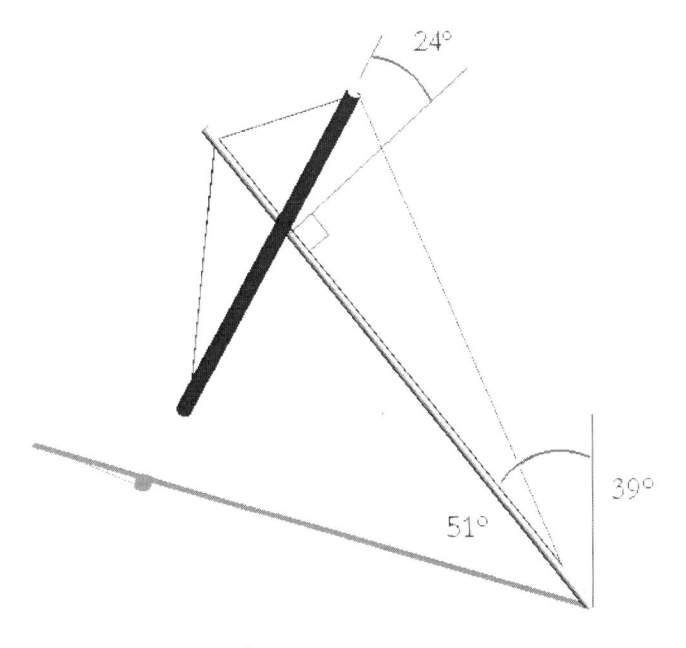

Summer arrangement

This experiment shows that the sun moves just like the stars with but one major exception; the sun appears to gradually change its position in the sphere: In high summer it is 24° up from the equatorial stars and in the depths of winter it has moved to 24° down.

The same experiment can be done further north. However, the angle between the ground and the stick gradually increases. To quickly check that the ground is not just sloping, the stick can be held by its end and gravity allowed to make it point down. If the angle of the polar axis changes when going north, a logical explanation is that the shape of the world must also be changing.

If the skies are probably the shape of a ball, is the Earth a ball too? The changing angle of the pole star, when travelling north, seems to indicate that it is. (Although it is not possible to see the curvature of the Earth at ground level, ships disappear over the horizon; also suggesting that the Earth is curved).

One way to test the idea is to find a high spot on an island far away from other land. The tip of a stick can be aligned with another so that both tips meet with the horizon. When looking back from the other stick, if both sticks still line up with the horizon the world must be flat and endless. However, if the second stick is above the horizon, the world is probably either a disc, a cylinder or a ball:

The World if a disc (courtesy of NASA)

But there is a problem with this experiment: When it is tried on a hill looking over sea, the horizon measured during the day is likely to be different from the one which appears when the sun sets (or when it rises). Haze can stop the real horizon from being seen:

Horizons: Haze in daytime and at sunrise

A way around this problem is to find a location where there is both a coastline jutting out into the sea and also a tall hill within that promontory. If the two sticks are aligned over sea with the morning sun, at the point where the horizon is in front of the sun, an exact line to the horizon can be found. After perhaps weeks or months, the sun will eventually set in exactly the opposite direction allowing the difference between angles to be found.

2: STONEHENGE AND THE HINGE 41

In a location which looks over sea, directly east and west, the whole experiment can be done on one day. At equinox, the sun rises in the east and sets in the west:

Aligning to sunrise

A high spot that works for this experiment is near Beachy Head at a place called Bourne Hill (about 200 metres above sea level). By chance, there is a Neolithic mound with an almost flat top in exactly the right location:

Aligning to sunrise using tripods as sticks

The experiment above shows that the shape of the world, looking east and west, is not flat. The experiment can be improved by making the mound into a dish with a level rim. Water will fill the dish when it rains and, if the dish is level, it will fill to the top without spilling. By making a level surface at the edge, downward angles at sunrise (in eastwards directions) can be compared to downward angles at sunset (westwards directions).

CGI image showing system

When this experiment is done, and provided the sun's rays can skim above water, the angle down to the sea horizon in front of the setting or rising sun proves to be the same in each direction. The unusually large Neolithic mound at Bourne Hill, perhaps by chance, is also shaped as a dish.

This last experiment only shows that the angles to the east and west are the same. It shows that the Earth is either a sphere-like object; or that the experiment itself is by chance at the centre of either a curved earth-disc or some type of cylinder (the change of angle going north shows that the world is curved from north to south). To find out which idea is right, the experiment could be done again at about the same height, but further along the coast: If the angles to the horizon start changing over these new sea views, the Earth could be a cylinder or a disc. If the angles never change (allowing for the height of each hill), the Earth is almost certainly a sphere.

There are other exceptionally good locations in Southern England for this experiment: St Catherine's (236m) is the tallest hill on the part of the Isle of Wight which juts out into the English Channel. At its summit there is also an unusually large Neolithic mound which appears to be bowled or flattened on top (scheduled monument no 459799). [01]

By doing the experiment on both the Isle of Wight and at Bourne Hill, the world on which we live can be shown to be curved like a sphere in all directions. Further along the coast in Dorset, the experiment could be done again at a 203m high point known as Swyre Head, where the coastline also juts out. Curiously, an unusually large Neolithic bowl tumulus also exists at this high point (scheduled monument no 456525).

2: STONEHENGE AND THE HINGE 43

With a few simple experiments, the world can be shown to be round, although it can not be said for certain what the other side of the world looks like. The world below appears to be solid and fixed, so if the assumption is made that the Earth is fixed, the axis of rotation of the moving heavens can be drawn relative to a picture of a fixed ball. The Sun, appearing to change its orbit from winter to summer, can also be drawn:

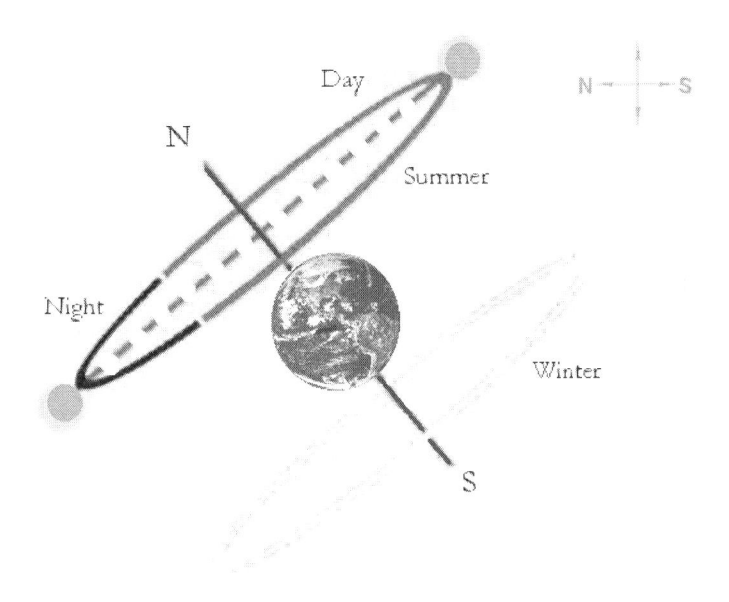

A drawing of apparent geocentric movement of the sun.

The most likely explanation for the heavens is that they too are round, but as yet no proof is available to show how big the heavens are.

The Hinge of the Heavens

The hinge of the heavens and the discovery of the world being a sphere would probably be important enough to draw out.

The angle of the hinge can be found by pointing a stick at the North Star. Looking at the world side-ways, a picture of a geocentric Universe can be drawn the most easily if east represents 'up' rather than north: The rotation of the stars around the pole can then be drawn as a big circle to indicate the rotating sphere of the heavens.

An observer at Stonehenge who is looking east (represented as a dot on the top of the ball in the picture below) can see the North Star at about 39° anti-clockwise from a line drawn straight up to the skies (vertical). The equatorial band of stars rotate at about 51° clockwise from vertical (the dashed line) and the sun also seems to orbit like the stars, but is up to 24° above the equator in summer and up to 24° down in winter:

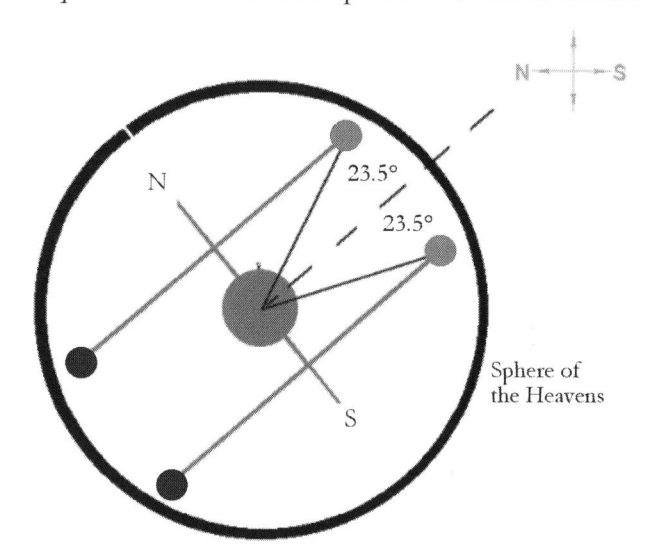

Drawing the Universe: England at the top of the world

The image above, *with an observer in England standing on the top of a ball*, shows one of the simplest geocentric explanations of our world, the heavens and how they appear to move around us.

A vertical line drawn at Salisbury, England (a latitude of about 51°), is one seventh of a circle from the equator (51°/360°) and 6/56ths from the polar axis (39°/360°). So the circle of the stars, showing the blackness of the sphere beyond, can be neatly divided into fifty six parts:

2: STONEHENGE AND THE HINGE   45

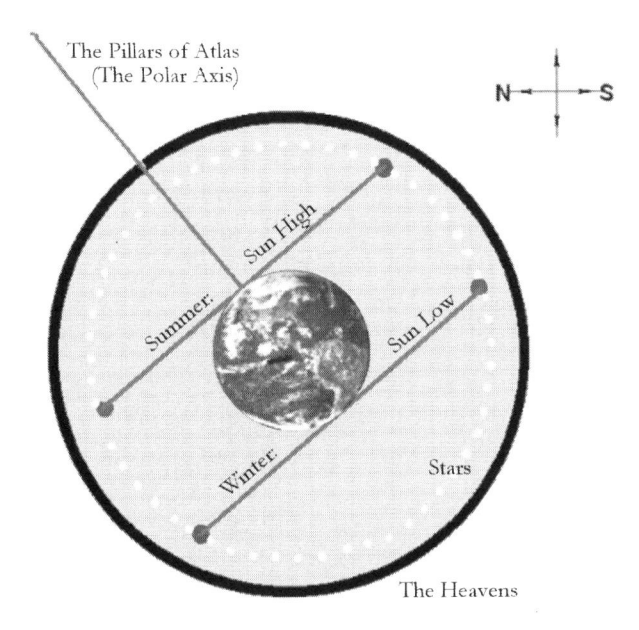

The 56 divisions of the heavens from Southern England (top).

This image (above) now duplicates Stonehenge's ground plan, with the stone circle representing the fixed ball of rock at the centre of the Universe:

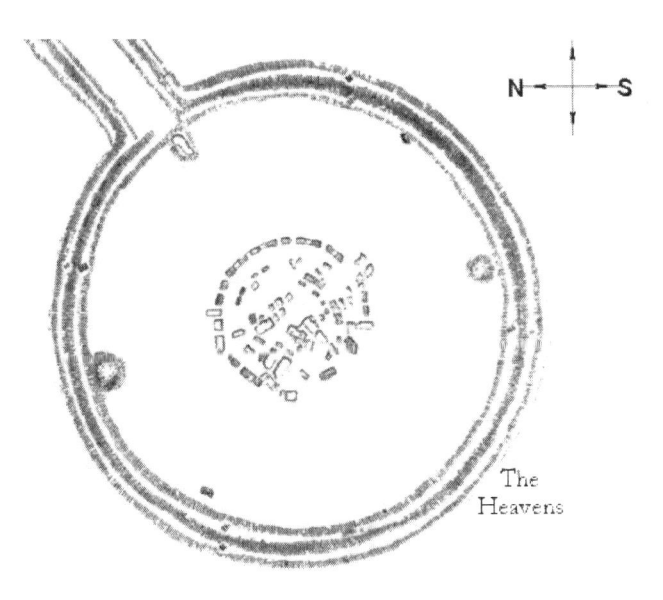

Modified & updated version of Stonehenge 1845 ground plan

To draw this image accurately, the direction of east or some other cardinal axis needs to be found. A very long straight pole could be pointed towards the North Star and a plumb-bob dropped to find north. However this is a lot of work, even if a straight tree trunk happens to be handy, and it only works well when a North Star is easy to find.

As described earlier, another way to find the east-west line is to go up to somewhere like Beachy Head and to find equatorial stars. Any of this band of equatorial stars, set close to what is known as the celestial equator, can subsequently be used to find an east-west line elsewhere. Providing the horizon can be seen to either the east or the west, the east-west line can be found by tracking one of these stars down to the horizon.

Stars seen rising and descending along the same set/rise line can also be used to find the days when the sun circles above the equator. On these days (known as equinox), two sticks aligned to sunset and sunrise will be almost perfectly aligned to east-west.

However, if the horizon is behind hills, the sun (or tracked stars) will set earlier than expected. The effect on setting out, if a west horizon is used to find east-west, is that the east-west line will appear to be rotated anti-clockwise from where it would have been had the hills not been in the way.

The path of the setting sun

A way around this is a method known as the Indian Circle:[02] A big circle is drawn around a stick on flat ground. When the sun rises, the end of the stick's shadow will touch the circle. When it sets, the shadow will touch the circle again for a second time. A line drawn between the two gives the east-west direction.

2: STONEHENGE AND THE HINGE   47

This is a useful counter-check but there is a potential problem: If the ground is not as flat as thought, and say slopes down from west to east, the shallow early morning shadow and will touch the raised edge of the circle earlier than it would had the ground been flat (because the sun is at a lower elevation). In the evening, with the western sun at a steeper angle, the shadow will touch the lowered eastern edge earlier than it should.

These two effects result in the same type of error which would be made when using a horizon which is raised by hills: If the ground slopes up to the west, the east-west line will appear to be rotated round anti-clockwise. If the ground slopes up to the east, the east-west line will appear to be rotated clockwise.

At a location like Stonehenge, where the east horizon is blocked by hills, the west, which appears to be flat to the horizon, makes an ideal setting out choice. The ground is also very flat at this particular location allowing the Indian Circle to be used for checking.

Unfortunately, these are both illusions: The horizon to the west is raised (there are hills in the far distance, particularly directly to the west). These hills raise the elevation by just under one degree above horizontal, which itself is slightly raised relative to the sea's horizon.

The ground at Stonehenge is also not as flat as it appears: It slopes down from west to east.[03] At Stonehenge's latitude, if the sky was drawn with east representing 'up', a drawing of the heavens with 56 divisions of latitude would be rotated anti-clockwise by about two degrees or so:

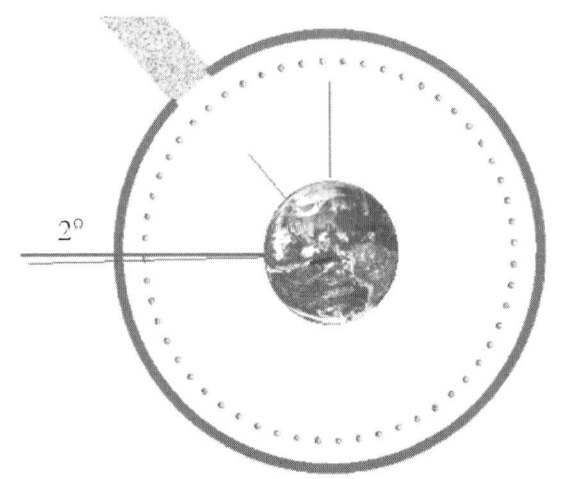

Setting out the heavens at Salisbury: East at top of picture

The original features of Stonehenge, before stone was brought onto the site, become identical when compared: The 56 Aubrey holes at Stonehenge are rotated anti-clockwise from cardinals by a couple of degrees. A circular bank surrounds them. The Avenue extends out at about one degree anti-clockwise from 39° (the ideal polar axis line). The southern entry also appears to be slightly out, anti-clockwise from south.

The original layout of Stonehenge therefore appears to fit a drawing of the world, and its Universe, when set out using the simplest methods available.

The sun's apparent winter and summer orbits can be laid onto an 'east=up' drawing and stone markers used to show the extent of the sun's movement. Four orbit points are needed to show both midday and midnight at the winter solstice and the same for the summer solstice. These four orbit points, which define the sun's movement, are in the same place as Stonehenge's four Station Stones (the drawing below shows the arrangement viewed from the west with east at the top):

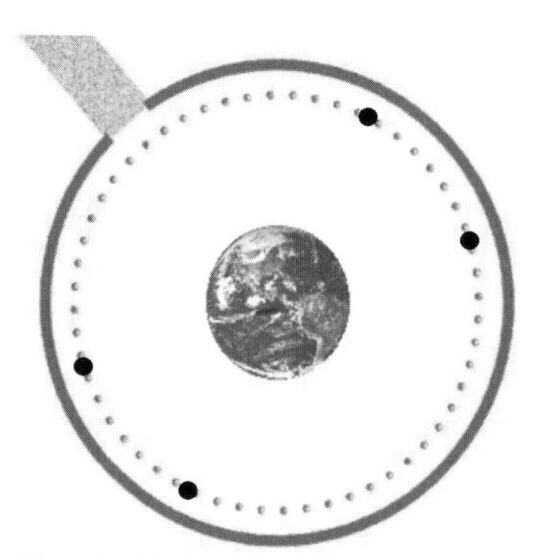

The sun's orbits in a geocentric Universe: (East at top)

This representation is now similar to Stonehenge's earlier original layout:

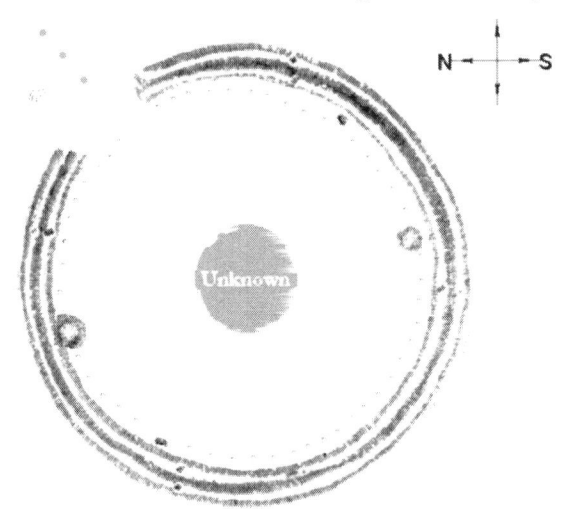

Modified version of Stonehenge 1845 Ground plan

The Sun appears to orbit the Earth whilst slowly moving by about 24° either side of the equatorial circle. This movement divides neatly into 30 parts (360/12) but not into the 56 latitudes of the heavens. A ring of 30 stones could instead be added to represent the Earth and to show the Sun's mathematical relationship to it. If this image is turned round by 90°, so that north is at the 'top', (the way we usually arrange maps today), this map of the Universe becomes identical to Stonehenge's final layout:

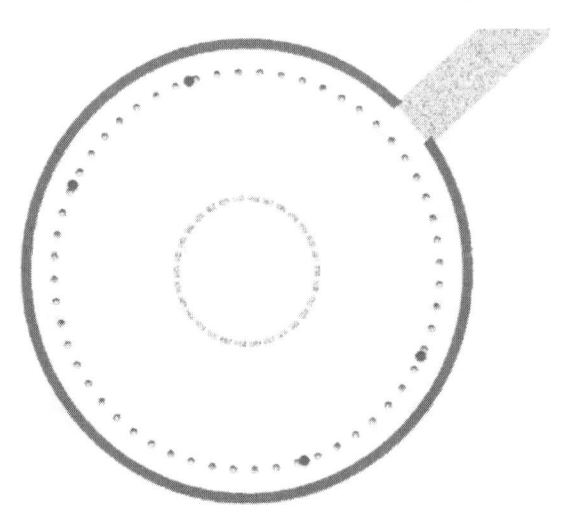

The Earth and solar markers: (North at top)

If the previous method of drawing were part of Stonehenge's original design, the layout would originally have been one or two degrees out of alignment. Other than bringing a huge tree-pole into the area, lining it up with the North Star and dropping a plumb line down to the centre of the circle, there is little or no way to see if a mistake has been made. And the idea that a tree-pole would have been brought into Stonehenge seems somewhat unlikely.

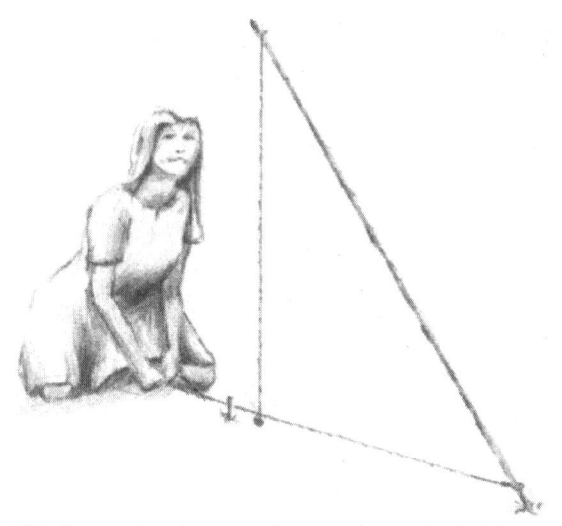

Finding north using a north-star pole & plumb-bob

But around about the time that Stonehenge was built, some of the Avenue's Stones seem to have been removed. The ones known to have been kept are the Heel-stone and the Slaughter-stone. At about the time the sarsen ring was built, a ditch was dug around the Heel-stone (after its counter-part stone had been removed), showing that the removal of stones was intentional.

These two remaining, or possibly repositioned, stones are in exactly the correct position to represent the real position of the polar axis relative to the true cardinal directions (north, south, east and west): If these two stones might represent a sudden increase in knowledge of how to find cardinal directions, the implication is that a more advanced method would have been used to set out the stones. But when the horizon is elevated by hills and magnets are not available, the only good method to obtain a precise cardinal layout is to trace a line to the North Star.

2: STONEHENGE AND THE HINGE

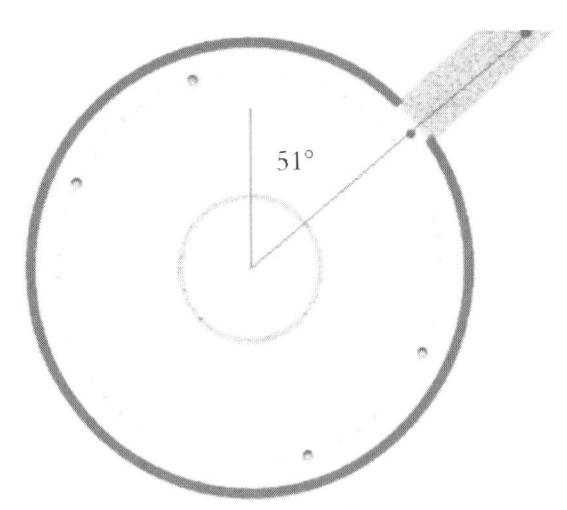

The Avenue stones which were kept (Heel & Slaughter)

A straight tree pole aligned with the Pole Star, (Thuban at that time), could have been placed so that a plumb-bob is dropped to the centre of the circle. When the shadow from that pole aligns with the plumb-bob (which only happens at midday), a very precise setting to true north can be found. This would be sufficiently accurate to show previous misalignments:

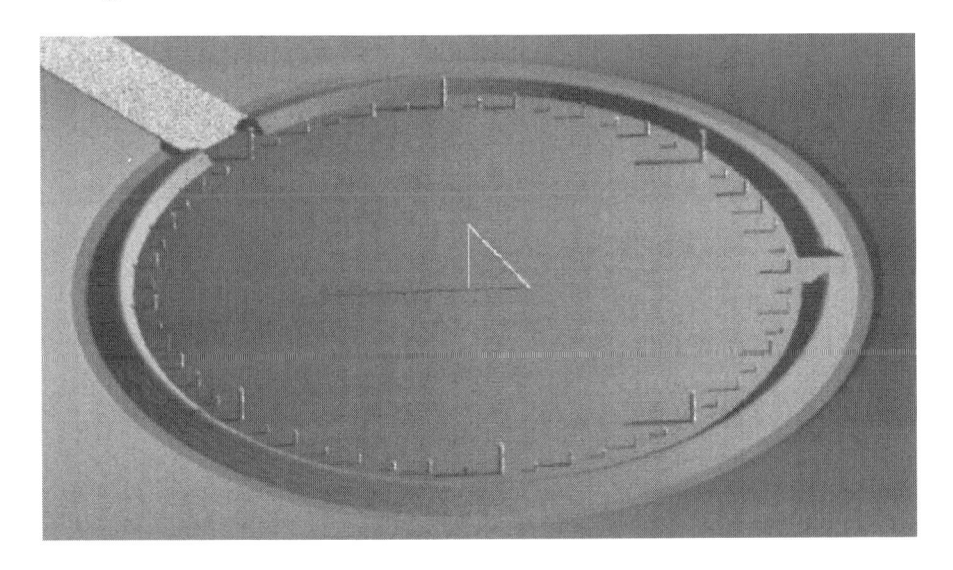

But if a tree pole was brought to Stonehenge, why was it brought in?

A special device in a geocentric Universe

The device which could be used to find the North Star, a stick pointing to the North Pole, can also be used with a sail-stick so that the sail traces a non-equatorial star (or even our own Sun). The image below shows a stick arranged to point to the sun at high summer from a position with a latitude of 51°:

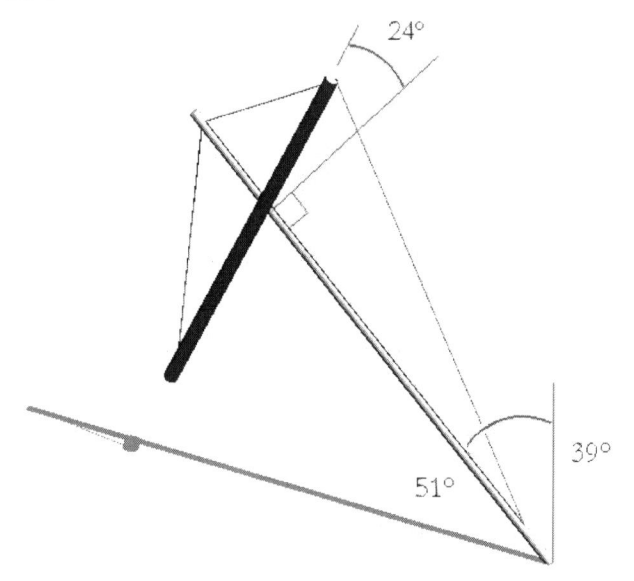

To trace the summer sun on a geocentric world

Whilst there is no evidence that a tree was brought into Stonehenge, there is a socket at the base of Stone 54 which is the right size to fit a tree. It is also the right shape. The low socket on Stone 54 is also directly south of the centre of the monument and is in exactly the correct location to work.

However, this large socket seems exceptionally well-worn; almost as if it had been damaged by constant re-installation. This does not fit with the idea of it being used for the construction of the monument.

The principle of a polar axis at 51° from horizontal, together with a rotating arm to track stars, was used at Greenwich Observatory to create what are known as the Equatorial Group of telescopes. When these telescopes are at right-angles to the support axis, they track equatorial stars;

2: STONEHENGE AND THE HINGE 53

An equatorial telescope at Herstmonceux, Sussex

The same idea can also be used to demonstrate how the Sun appears to rotate around our world: From the top of a fixed ball, with the top representing Southern England, the Sun can be shown to disappear from view at night:

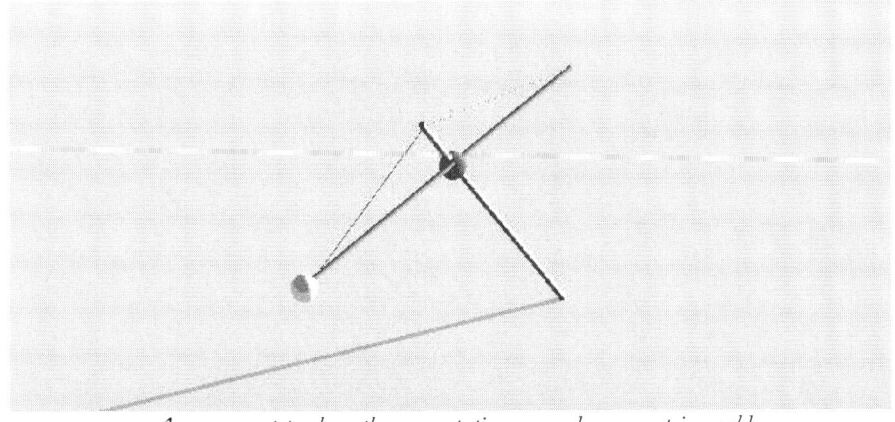

Arrangement to show the sun rotating around a geocentric world

Before Stonehenge was conceived, it seems that tin and copper had been discovered.

Tin is a material which reflects light. It can also be easily moulded to shape using an ordinary fire.

Cast tin after cooling

After casting, it can be polished using chalk paste (powder combined with water or oil) to make a mirror.

Cast tin after hand polishing using chalk paste

Tin degrades if it is kept in a cold climate (a process known as 'tin pest'). Unlike almost all other metals, it gradually turns to dust over centuries giving no evidence that it had ever been used. Unfortunately, this effect means that the discovery of tin mirrors in archaeological digs would be exceptionally unlikely.

Crude tin mirrors have a reflectivity greater than 50% and can easily be used to reflect a bright light onto a ball. The idea of using reflected light could then be used to improve a demonstration which shows how the Sun seems to rotate around the Earth:

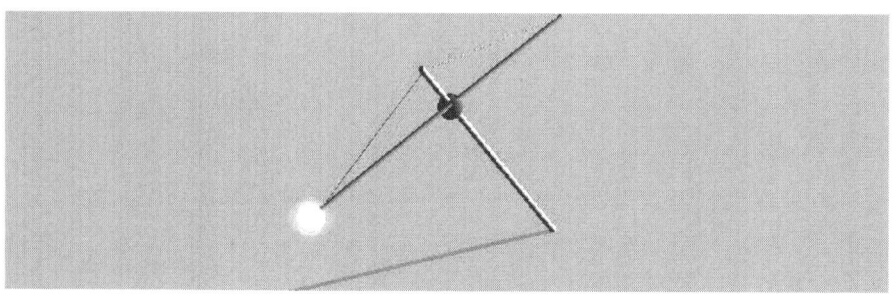

Using mirrors to light up a model of a geocentric sun

The problem with using reflections to light up a sun-ball is that the mirrors have to be constantly re-focused to keep track of reflections as the sun moves.

Adjusting the mirrors

However, if the mirrors are arranged as a sphere and the sail rotated, (rather than moving the mirrors), the mirrors will remain automatically focused for several hours providing the sail is set at the correct length:

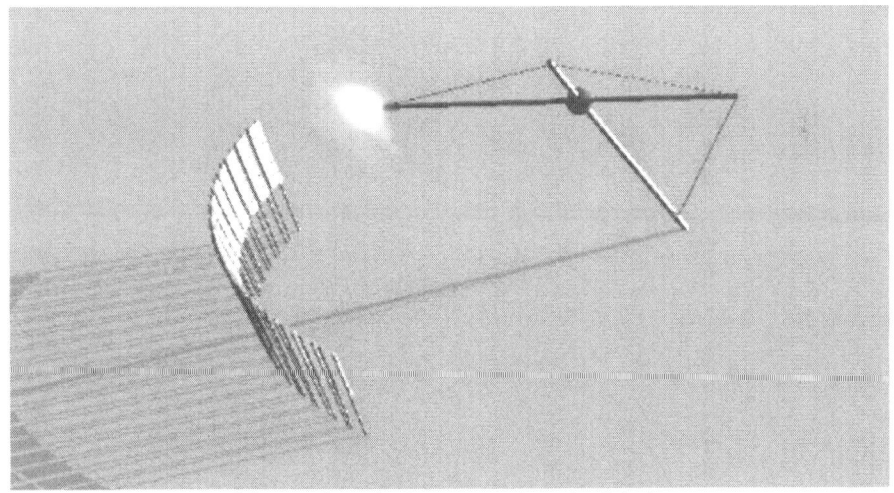

Using spherical mirrors to make a focal device

The effect of spherical concentration is used at the Aceribo Observatory[04] where a giant spherical collector has been arranged to collect radio waves from distant galaxies.

When used in a demonstration device, sets of spherical mirrors have to be kept tightly in place so that they do not move in the wind. An inwardly facing cylinder, a circle of very strong material, is therefore required at high level together with flat faces against which the mirrors can be measured and tied.

To ensure that the mirror sets form a sphere, which has the same centre for all of the mirrors, this circle of strong material also needs a perfectly level rim:

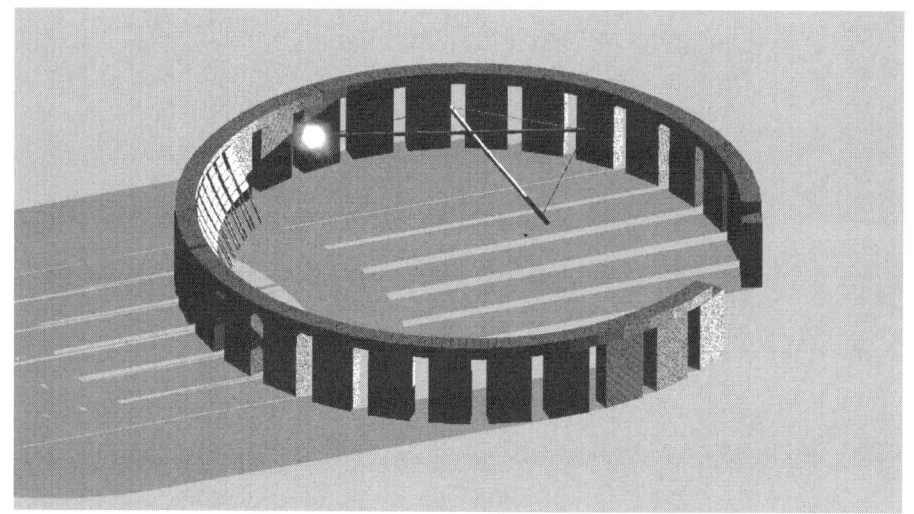

The setting ring: To support winter mirrors

At Stonehenge there is a high level ring of inwardly facing lintels arranged as a shallow cylinder. Due south of the centre of this circle, a stone pair (stone 53 and 54) have a socket into which a tree could be inserted. If the tree were pointed at the North Star, and a second pole rotated around it, mirrors placed against the lintel rim would focus light to a ball.

As the sun rises in its circle, the ball descends along the path of a circle. As the sun sets, the ball rises. If a demonstration were needed of how the sun moves in a Universe believed to be geocentric, this is the perfect arrangement.

However, tin and copper were newly discovered materials. They were probably more valuable than gold is today and would not be left out overnight. Metals would need to be stored in a safe place, moved to location in the morning, and then set up so that they focus.

This arrangement would therefore only be ideal for afternoon use when the ball appears to be rising. To reflect, mirrors need to face the sun. In Southern England, the sun travels from south to west over the course of an afternoon. Therefore mirrors must be placed in the north east with their reflections bounced up onto the ball; now rising to the north east of the centre.

The best place to see this effect would be from the north east: A wide avenue, such as the Avenue north east of Stonehenge, would be ideal to show the effect of a bright mini-sun to a huge number of people.

The three season device

The device described so far has a rod which points up by 24° in the winter. This allows the shining ball to appear just above the top of the supports. However, the arrangement described is only good for winter.

After winter passes, the sun gets higher in the sky. The rotating rod must point to the sun, so the end of the pole and its reflector must go down. At equinox (spring or autumn), the rod will be at right-angles to the pole. In summer, the sun is high, so the reflector-ball will be even lower.

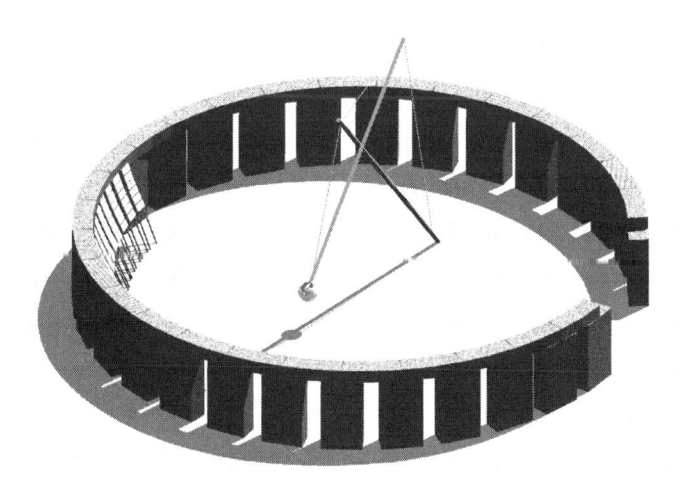

Summer: The sail pointing down

The effect of this, after winter passes, is that the focal point (on the ball) disappears below the top of the mirrors when viewed from the outside:

One way to improve this design is to raise the axis by just enough so that the whole assembly is again visible above the ring. As summer approaches, the whole assembly can be raised for a second time:

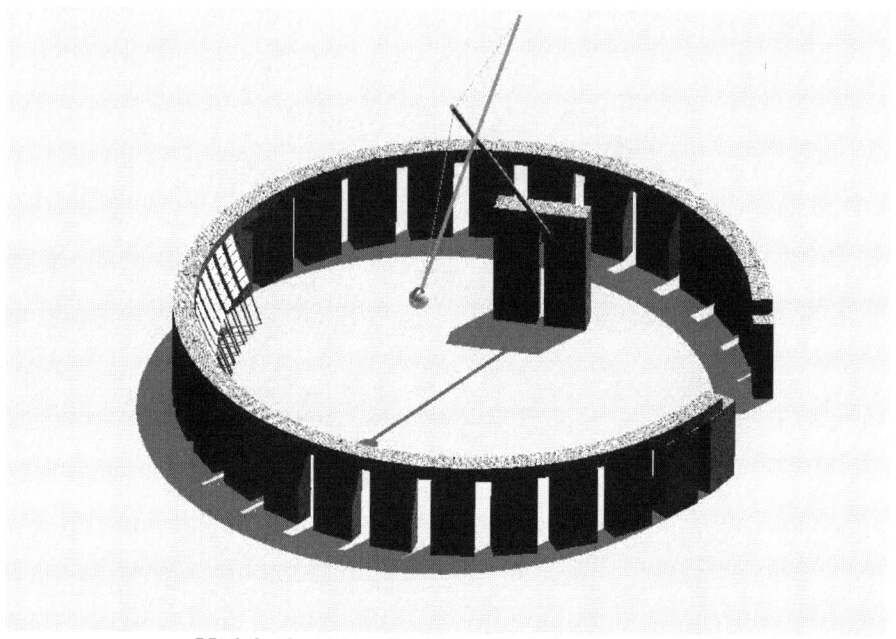

High level position of the 3-season socket arrangement

When dimensions are calculated, it proves to be possible to position the pole so that the ball of light is always in the correct position above the rim of circular stone.

A pole is very light by comparison to the heaviest stone (stone 54) at Stonehenge.[05] It can be lifted and hauled to its final position, a little like a May Pole, using the counter-balance of the stone's weight:

Mid May; the first day of summer: Raising the Maypole

2: STONEHENGE AND THE HINGE 59

And the pole position and angle set using a plumb-bob and marker located earlier using a smaller pole set to the North Star:

Setting the angle and location

To make this work at Stonehenge, two extra sockets would be needed so that the assembly can be moved up.

At Stonehenge, two extra sockets appear to exist on stone 54. These are in exactly the positions required to allow the shining light to rise above the lintels in any season. The holes also appear to be the right shape and orientation.

Stones 53 and 54: Stonehenge

A second effect of moving the assembly up is that the mirrors must be moved over and then tilted so that the spherical centre moves up with the apparatus: In summer, the mirrors are highly angled so are easy to prop from the ground. But at equinox, a second set of low-level supports would be best introduced, just inside the main ring, to prop the tilted and shifted mirrors:

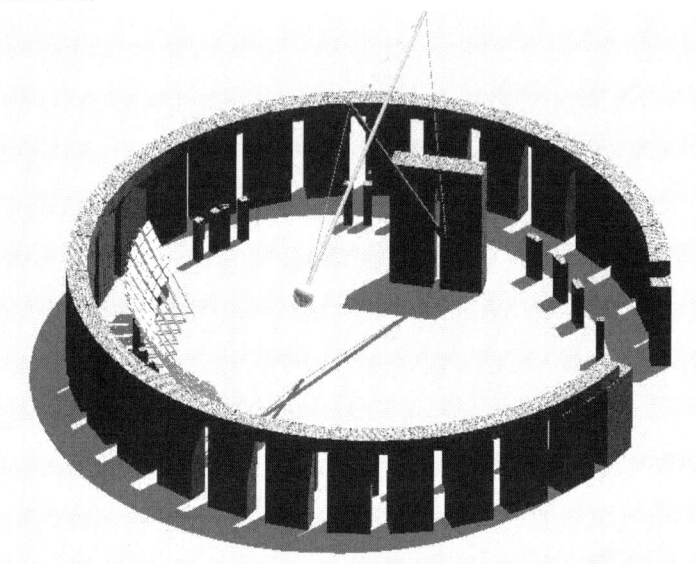

The equinox support requirement; Bowl centre raised by 2 metres

At Stonehenge, a second ring of stones, known as the outer bluestone circle, exists in just the right place to provide solid support points for mirrors which are tilted and shifted for spring or autumn:

The outer bluestone circle

2: STONEHENGE AND THE HINGE   61

The rotating collector is heavier at one end than it is the other. To improve the design, either a counterweight can be hung off the end or the end can be tied down to a series of holding down posts:

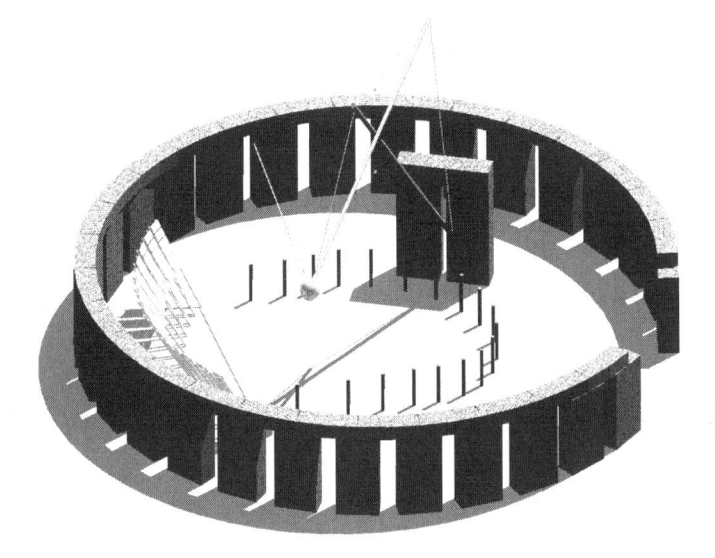

Oval or horse-shoe counterweight ring

At Stonehenge, another set of stones exists in just the right place to allow the high end of the rotating pole to have either a counterweight guide or to be tied down. These stones are known as inner bluestones:

Stonehenge's inner bluestones

To allow the rotator to be hauled around the polar axis and firmly tied against wind, tall and strong platforms are needed in the north east, arranged so that they do not cast too much shadow on the mirrors. To enable the fitting of a reflector, the end of the sail must be accessible from these platforms in winter:

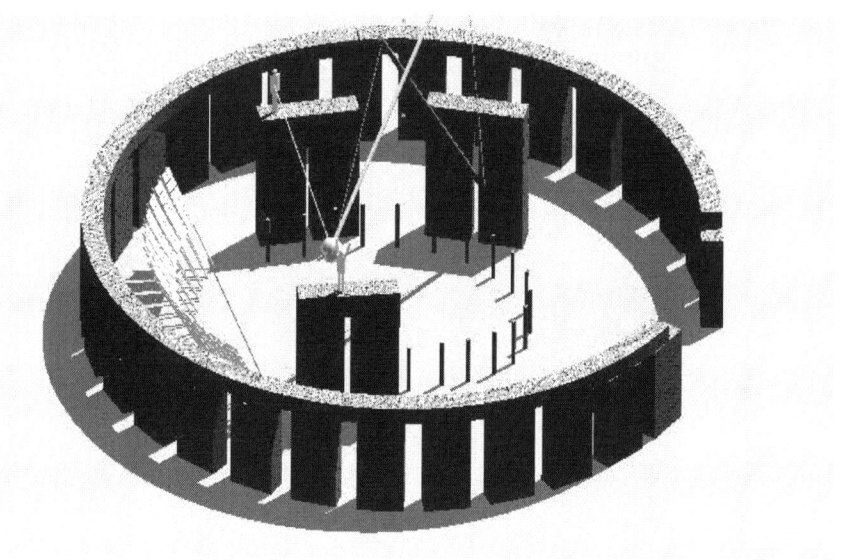

Adding the loading and rotation platforms

At Stonehenge, two sets of trilithons (Stones 51&52 and Stones 59&60) are set in just the right position to allow the sail to be rotated, be restrained against the occasional gust of wind, give access to the reflector and not cast too much shadow on the north east mirrors.

However, when the pole is raised by one level for either the spring or autumn, the end of the sail is only just reachable (so that it can be fitted with a reflector): In summer, with the pole two levels up, the reflector is far too high to allow access to the end of the rotating arm.

A way to get around this is to install two extra sets of platforms so that the end of the sail can be reached no matter which position the pole is placed in. Because these must be higher platforms than the two used at the north east, they need to be set at the back so that they cast the least amount of shadow:

2: STONEHENGE AND THE HINGE 63

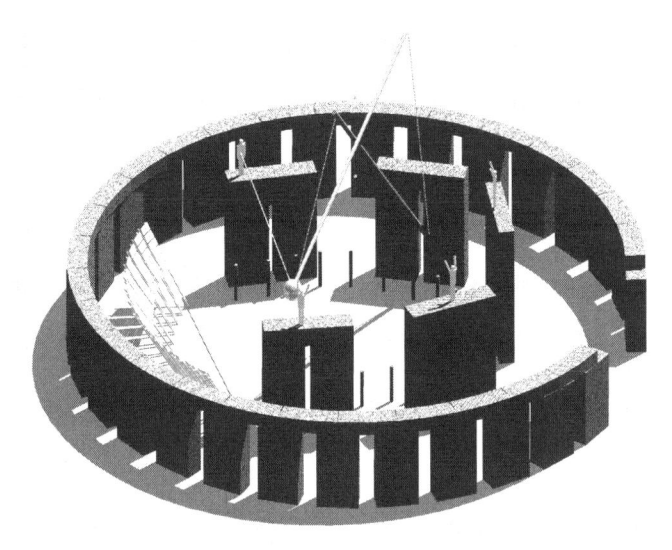

Adding platforms for equinox and summer

At Stonehenge, two sets of trilithons (Stones 55&56 and Stones 57&58) exist at just the right position and height to allow these operations to occur.

The three season device creates a ball of light. The ball appears to glide on a sunbeam because its sail always points towards the sun. As clouds appear, the ball would turn dull and with each new ray of sunshine it would light up:

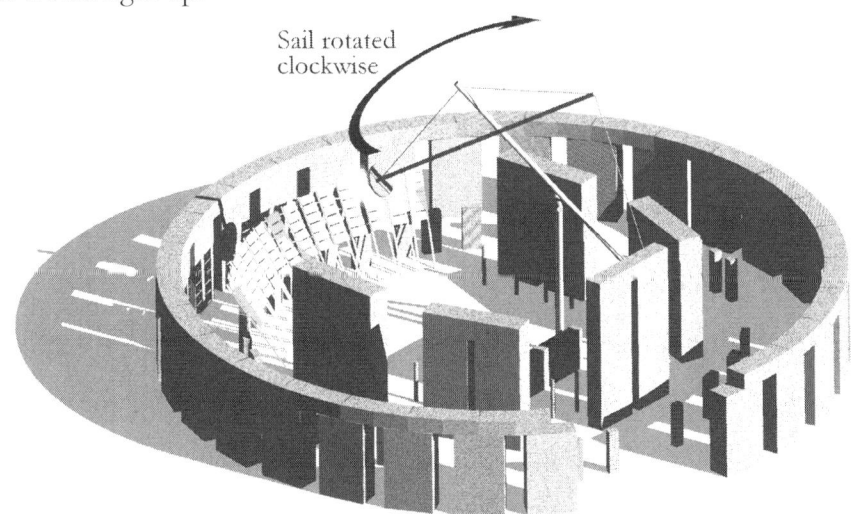

Rotation of the sail

The reflector can be a number of shapes. It can also be made to concentrate light in certain directions, but the overall effect is to create a small version of the sun which appears to rise on the sail towards the heavens.

View from the north east

Decay

Most modern structures are facilities which are designed to contain or carry other things. For example, a museum's purpose is related to its contents, but the contents will always be the first thing to be removed when the building becomes outdated or threatened.

A solar structure of the type described here contains two sets of temporary features: The first set of temporary features are the mirrors and the reflector, both containing metal; a precious commodity. Additional temporary structure (such as the pole, ladders, ramps and so on) forms the second set.

At the time Stonehenge was constructed, the metal components would have been more valuable than a structure such as Stonehenge. Containing and using metal would have been the primary purpose of a building designed to be a solar concentrator. As with a museum, these valuable contents would be the first to be removed if the structure either fell into disuse or came under threat of pillage. In the unlikely event that any metal was left behind, tin would gradually crumble to dust over the centuries leaving no trace other than an elevated tin content within the soil.

The second set of temporary features (ladders, ropes, poles, platforms and so on) might be left in place in the event of a sudden fall into disuse. Because these items are less valuable, they could also be stored nearby. Either way, timber left above ground eventually rots and thus returns to the soil leaving no trace.

In other words, the structure described in this introduction would leave no trace other than the structure which currently exists at Stonehenge.

Summary

When the sun leaves the far north in winter, the land becomes cold. On a world believed to be geocentric, the sun turns with the celestial sphere but appears to have a will of its own. Knowledge of how the heavens work could therefore have been seen as fundamental to the continued existence of people living at the edges of the world.

Stonehenge's plan layout can be shown to be the same as an idealised geocentric description of the Universe. Its inner stone monument is demonstrated to be capable of producing a spectacular public display of solar movement. The arrangement of this system is shown to be based on a simple method of tracking celestial objects.

Therefore, Stonehenge could have been both a depository of knowledge about the Universe and a place of learning designed for popular interest.

3: THE SIZE OF THE WORLD

In the first part, Stonehenge was shown to be the same as an idealised geocentric description of the Universe; its inner stone monument capable of producing a spectacular public display of solar movement using reflected light. But Stonehenge is only a single monument; its apparent arrangement as a place to teach knowledge of the Universe could be just coincidental.

If a knowledge of the heavens was so well known that Stonehenge were built to teach and celebrate knowledge of the sun, there would be traces elsewhere of the experiments used to find that knowledge:

> Knowledge of how the sun and the heavens revolve;
> The ideas used to explore what the world might be;
> The systems used to prove that knowledge;
> The methods used to explain what was being done.

The second part of this introduction shows more of the ideas about the world which lie behind the storyline of the novel. When I started looking for locations to show this, the idea was just to prove that these things could have been done, not that they had been done. I selected locations using topographical maps and then carried surveying kit up along the paths of the South Downs to test the ideas. However, on arrival I found Neolithic monuments all arranged as if designed for the purpose: The surveying equipment was unnecessary.

In this part, monuments in East Sussex are used to show that Old World enquiry into the nature of the Universe could easily have produced a science based on the ideas of a geocentric world.

The photographs shown are of real places and tests. A place for students to perhaps learn about how to study the world; an introduction before going to Stonehenge.

The idea

On a curved world, it should be possible to see the world's curvature from a hill by finding the slope down to the horizon. On a very tall mountain, the angle down to the horizon will be easy to see:

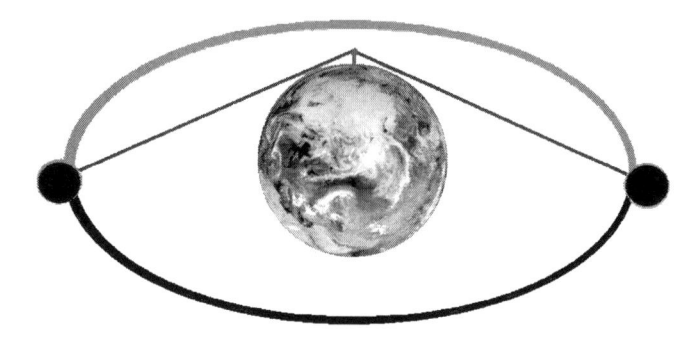

Seeing the curvature of the Earth using the Sun

If the Earth seems to be a ball, is it possible to work out its size using only wood and the land?

Twice per year, the sun rises directly in the east and then sets directly in the west. At this time of year (equinox), the difference between the angle at sunrise and then sunset can be measured using two sticks:

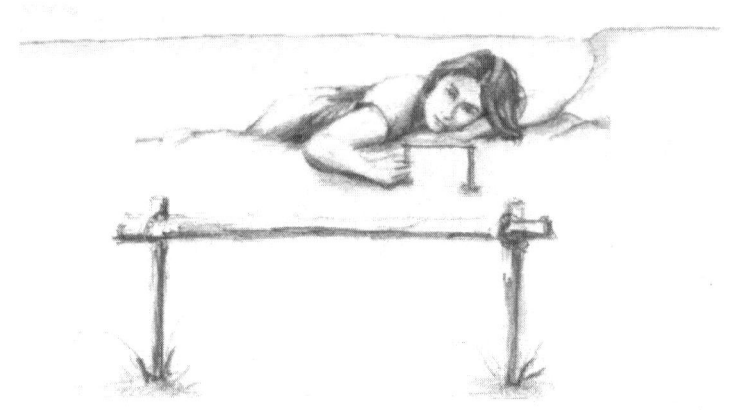

Using sticks as horizon sight-lines

3: THE SIZE OF THE WORLD

At sunrise or sunset on a clear day, the horizon is not obscured by haze. Looking over sea views at the far tip of south eastern England, there is an ancient hill-top ridge where this discovery could easily have been made by chance:

The highest hilltop ridge adjacent to Beachy Head

This small ridge is some 165 metres above sea level and adjacent to the cliffs of Beachy Head. It is also adjacent to the ancient track known as the South Downs Way.

Using the rates of cliff erosion below the nearby Bell Tout lighthouse, the cliff would have been some 400 metres or so further south in Neolithic times.[01] Nevertheless, this ridge could be used for discovery today in the same way as it could have 5000 years ago.

Finding a hill's height

Next to cliffs of Beachy Head, the easiest way to find the height above sea is drop a rope down. Because the geological bedding of the chalk is horizontal, the cliffs overhang high tide allowing very accurate measurement:

The cliffs near Beachy Head

Another method is to use a level, for instance a water-filled trough cut into timber, to sight onto a pole stood on lower ground. The height between one spot and another can be found by sighting horizontally over the water in the trough.

A level such as this is not very accurate but could work well over short distances. However, it would be too inaccurate for long distance work.

Using a trough as a level

This process can be repeated all the way down a hill, each time adding the difference in height to get a total.

This second method could also work well near Beachy Head, where the seafront is just over a kilometre away along the eastern paths which lead at a gentle slope to Eastbourne's seafront:

Looking east from Beachy Head

At Beachy head, looking north over the downs, there are several other hills which are obviously higher and could give better accuracy for experiments:

The hills to the north of Beachy Head

Bourne Hill, the nearest high point, is also sited next to the South Downs Way and has a very large flat topped tumulus which looks both east and west over sea views:

Bourne Hill Tumulus

One method of finding a height, mentioned earlier, is to sight horizontally to the top of a pole and to drop a measuring line down. The same system of sighting to the next pole can then be used downhill and over long distances.

This process is just like using a builder's level but on a very large scale. However, it needs a more accurate horizontal sight-line than a water filled trough. One other method is to use a level mound of several metres diameter, perhaps constructed as a dish to collect water: When filled to the brim on a still day, the edges can be checked so that they are perfectly level.

A ring has a number of advantages compared to a long trough: Once constructed, it no longer needs to have any water and it can be used to sight in any direction. This second advantage means that anyone can check the ring at a later date. Though a ring-platform with a finely finished top surface is useful for surveying, it is unlikely that the same reasons for constructing one would exist in many other locations.

In a location such as the eastern hills of the South Downs, which are right next to the sea, the exactness of level can also be easily checked against the sea's horizon (below the horizontal sight-line). This could potentially give an accuracy as good as 0.02°, depending on the eyesight of the user.

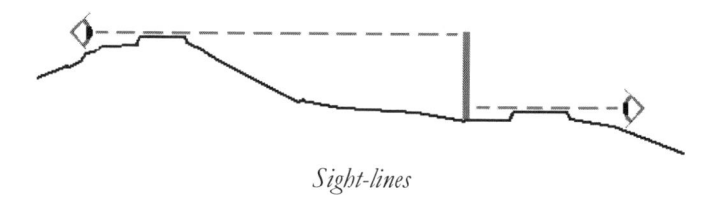

Sight-lines

However, there is a limitation: Up to about 12 metres, a shaved pine pole, perhaps 100mm diameter (weighing about 40kg) can be carried by two people. Anything bigger than this, though difficult to carry, could be used but on a more permanent basis.

Once lifted to an angle, a pole can be hauled up to position using rope and then tied to stakes. To get any higher than 12 metres probably needs a second thinner pole, hauled up to position using rope rather like a sail:

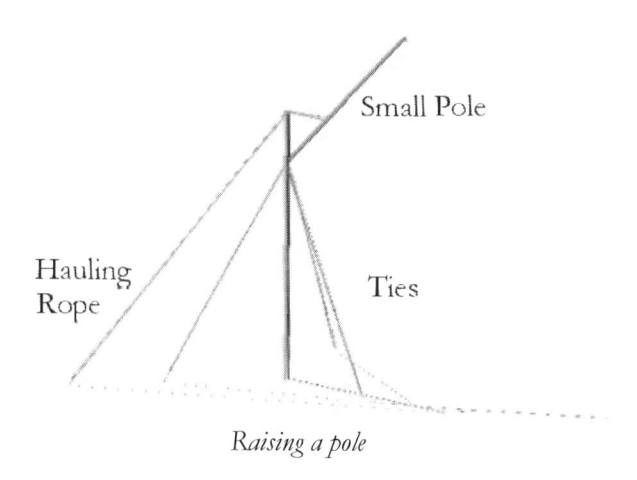

Raising a pole

3: THE SIZE OF THE WORLD

A second limitation is the height of local trees. Although it is possible that trees could have been allowed to grow taller in Neolithic times, trees today rarely grow to greater than about 25 metres in the nearby Friston Forest. This puts a limitation of about 20 metres, probably less, on the height difference that can be found between any two platforms.

From Bourne Hill (202m above sea) due south to the hills by Beachy Head, the shortest route is along the high ridge of the ancient track known as the South Downs Way. Along this track-way there are three intervening hill brows with a maximum distance between each of about 1.5 kilometres. These exist at the high points of Foxholes Brow (about 183m), Beachy Brow (about 168m) and Pashley Hill (about 167m).

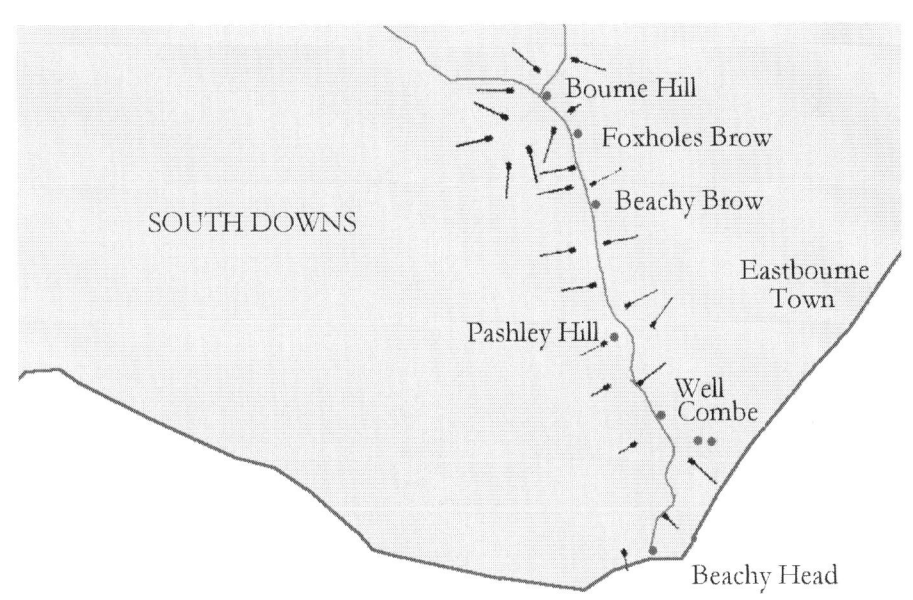

The route from Beachy Head to Bourne Hill

On each of these high points there exists at least one Neolithic bowl tumulus, typically about 8 metres diameter. Each of these is on a high point location which has direct views of both the sea and the other hill top tumuli in the series.

Foxholes Brow Tumulus:

Foxholes Brow bowl tumulus (one of two tumuli)

View of Bourne Hill from Foxholes Brow looking north

Beachy Brow Tumulus:

Beachy Brow bowl tumulus

View of Bourne Hill & Foxholes Brow from Beachy Brow

Each of these tumuli is ideally sized and located to provide an exceptionally accurate sighting platform to the next tumulus (or anything else) along the South Downs Way:

Sighting on a flat bowl

These Tumuli run all the way from Bourne Hill to Pashley Hill, where another sight-line goes to a Tumulus at Well Combe, followed by two more tumuli, each about 15-20 metres or so below the next. According to English Heritage, about 15-20 metres below the lowest of these two tumuli are the ploughed out remains of yet another possible tumulus (Monument 152278) set within a later prehistoric field system. Below this, all other remains are likely to have been destroyed.

The seven or eight tumuli described in this part[02] are just a small sample along this route. For example, between Bourne and Foxholes, there are three more tumuli, all arranged to have sight of others. Between Pashley Hill and Beachy Brow, there are another half dozen. All of these tumuli are along, or slightly set off, the South Downs Way.

The remains of tumuli along the South Downs Way, between Beachy Head and Bourne Hill, are all located in a way which would allow the height of Bourne Hill or other locations to be found with reasonable accuracy.

Location of other tumuli

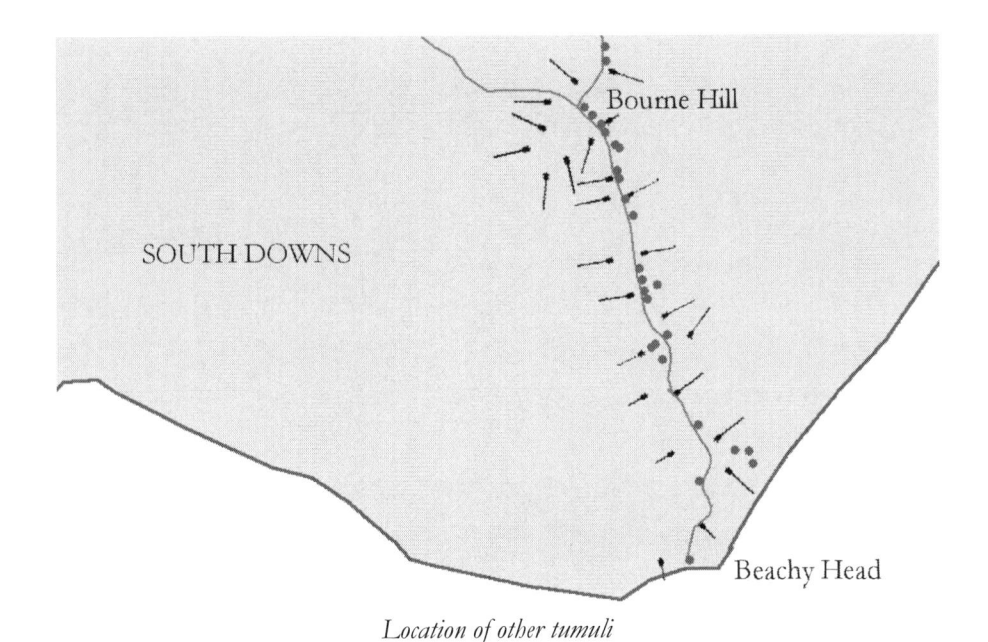

A modern experiment

It is possible to line up a horizontal bar so that it aligns to the horizon shown by the sun at equinox. To test the theory, I ran the experiment on Bourne Hill: Two sticks were adjusted so that they met the sunset at the moment the sun disappeared from the horizon:

After sunrise looking west

3: THE SIZE OF THE WORLD

When the sun rises, the sticks are not aligned with the horizon. The height difference was then measured:

Bourne Hill: Sunrise at equinox

In the above rough experiment at Bourne Hill (autumn equinox 2012), the measured height difference was just under 150mm (6") over a distance of just under 10 metres (about 32') giving a measured slope of about 1:130 in each direction.

The radius of a circle (R) measured using a shallow slope is approximately 2 x h / (Ø x Ø), where h is the height above the circle:

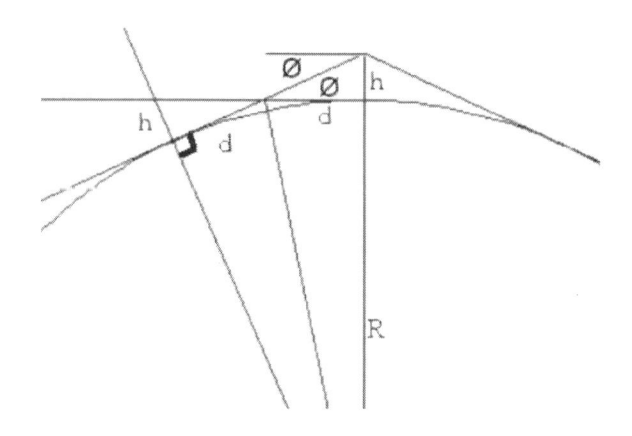

The angles needed for the mathematics

The approximate radius of the Earth (as measured using this rough experiment in June 2012) was within a few percentage points of the real size of our world.

A person with younger and sharper eyes than me should be able to see even better angular resolutions, especially if the whole width of the tumulus was used.

Calculating the size of the world

From Bourne Hill, another sight-line exists to a hill named Cold Crouch, a short walk away along a northern fork of the South Downs Way. On top of this high point (approx 182m) is a further Neolithic bowl tumulus. Between are two further tumuli on an intervening ridge named Babylon Down.

To the immediate north west of Cold Crouch, a singular unusually tall bowl tumulus exists at the summit of Combe Hill (193m):

Combe Hill: Tumulus A

This location, like all the other bowl tumuli in the area, has good sea views to the east and to the west.

The best way to visualise how this calculation works is to imagine being on the world, and seeing the Sun's angle down from horizontal in both the morning and afternoon:

3: THE SIZE OF THE WORLD 79

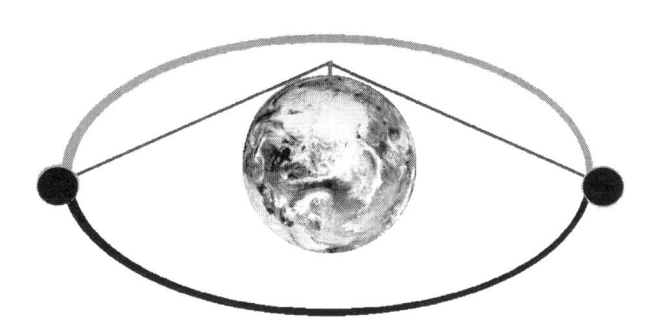

Seeing the curvature of the Earth using the Sun

If the above drawing is done to a large enough scale, and with large angles to demonstrate the principles, a person could sight onto a 'sun point' from a giant ball drawn on the ground and check that the size of the world really can be found by using twice the height divided by the square of the slope.

Curiously, just below the high bowl tumulus is a place known as the Combe Hill Camp, a one-off Neolithic structure in Sussex which is famously larger than Stonehenge: [03]

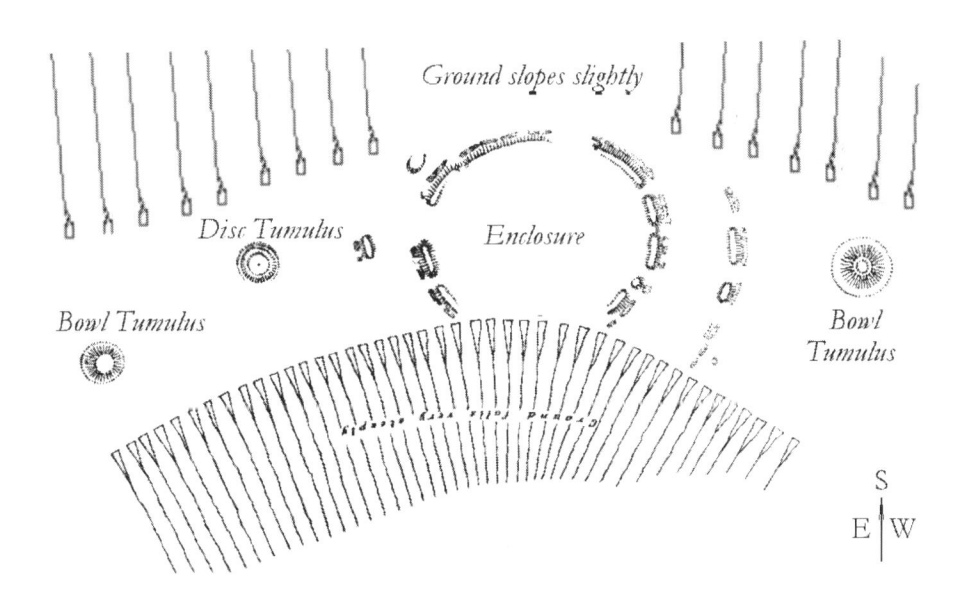

Adapted from Map by Curwen

This layout, perhaps by chance, is similar to the one used earlier to explain how to calculate the size of the Earth using the Sun's rays:

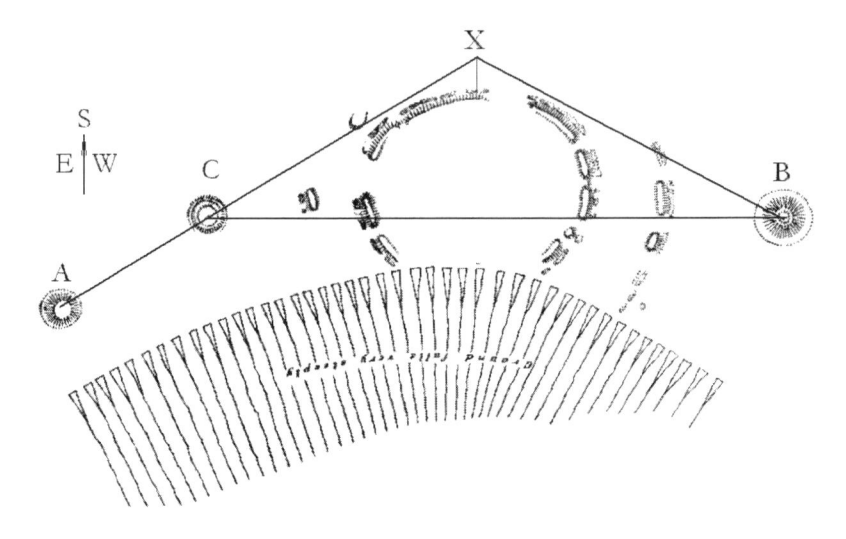

Showing how to calculate the curvature of the Earth

The line from 'X' crosses through a ring tumulus 'C' and sights onto tumulus 'A'. Bowl tumulus 'B' can also be seen from the top rim of the main circle:

Combe Hill: Bowl Tumulus B

Curiously, the angle which exists at Combe Hill is about 24°; the angle of the sun's furthermost change in apparent orbit (nowadays known as 'Axial Tilt'). This is also the angle described in the stones seen at Stonehenge.

The rotation of the Heavens

The path from Combe Hill leads down through an ancient field system to a village called Jevington, where it re-joins the current path of the South Downs Way coming from Bourne Hill. At the next stop along the South Downs Way, several more bowl tumuli exist at the brow of Folkington Hill. These tumuli also look directly east and west over sea views.

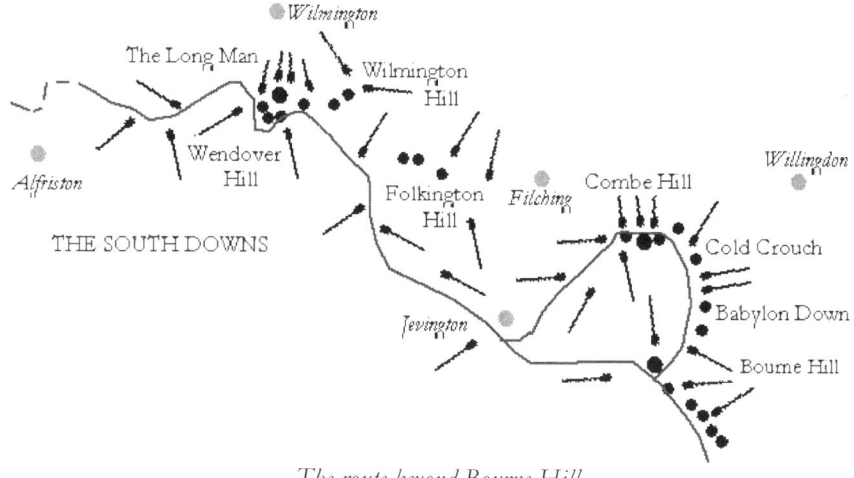

The route beyond Bourne Hill

Yet another bowl tumulus exists at the peak of the adjacent hill, Wilmington (213 metres). This too is located at a spot which has direct sea views to the east and west. By the time you have walked from Beachy Head to Wilmington Hill, you will probably have seen enough of bowl tumuli with direct sea views east and west which are situated on ridges within sight of other bowls along the same path.

A few hundred yards further west is yet another bowl-like tumulus at Windover Hill. This one is curiously unusual: It does not have particularly good sea views and its view to the east is obscured by Wilmington Hill.

Below this hill is an exceptionally steep north facing slope which points upwards at just the right direction to find the polar axis. Here you can lie comfortably on the ground at night and, using two sticks, follow the rotation of the stars. Perhaps by coincidence, the other nearby steep north facing slope is below the Combe Hill Camp.

This hill was cleared of trees in the Neolithic period. On the steep north facing slope of the hill is a figure of a man holding two sticks:

The Long Man, East Sussex

In the 16th century, the figure was lined using bricks. No-one knows who decided to turn the figure from a dusty chalk outline into a permanent figure.

By using two sticks over a long night, the stars can be seen to rotate in almost a full circle. The most obvious explanation for this, if the Earth is fixed, is that the Universe too is a sphere.

The unusual tumulus at the top of Windover Hill appears to have a notch in its north face which looks down over an amphitheatre, possibly natural, with a north facing bowl:

The Long Man's Amphitheatre (bowl tumulus seen at top right)

Curiously, its only entrance is directly north of the tumulus on the hilltop above. This amphitheatre is divided into two segments: The larger has a perfectly flat base and the smaller is arranged as a bowl. A second path leads up directly south along the reclining ridge which divides the two amphitheatres.

Though its age is unknown, this amphitheatre has steep north facing sides which allow comfortable viewing and demonstration of the rotation of the heavens.

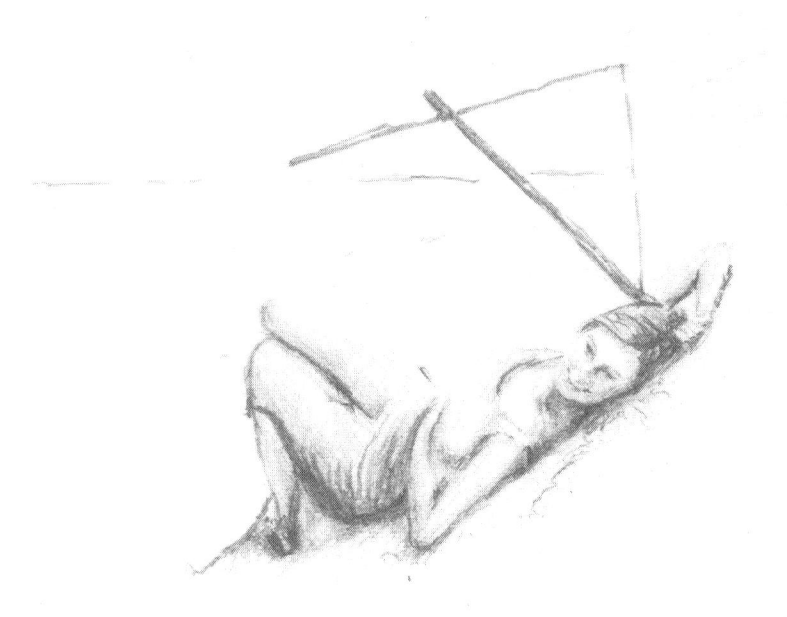

Following the rotation of the Heavens on a northern slope

At this latitude, very similar to that of Stonehenge, the stars rotate around an axis some 51° from horizontal. Curiously, a long barrow immediately adjacent to this amphitheatre points at an axis of some 51° east of north; the same direction as the Avenue at Stonehenge.

Summary

The area around Bourne Hill appears to be exceptionally well laid out to prove that the Earth is curved to find its size. Although there is no evidence that Bourne Hill was especially important to the local area, it is curious that the district of the large town to the east is named "Eastbourne": The archaic word Bourne can mean destination or goal.[04]

The tumuli leading from Beachy Head to Bourne Hill have the appearance of being laid out as sighting platforms to allow the height at any point along the route to be measured. There are dozens of Neolithic man-made platforms along this route. Many of these also appear to be arranged as the Bourne Hill experiment to allow it to be shown to many people (as well as providing an accurate height measurement for adjacent platforms). If this area's purpose were to teach, the layout and number of monuments indicates that this was done on a vast scale.

The area around Combe Hill has the appearance of being laid out to show how to calculate the size of the world. The angle used appears to be the same as the angle of the Earth's axial tilt. This is a simple calculation to demonstrate at any time of day, allowing a very large number of people to see how it works with just the one layout.

The Long Man monuments appear to be laid out to demonstrated the rotation of the heavens about the polar axis. Though there is no evidence that the polar axis was important to the area, it is curious that the district surrounding the Long Man is named "Polegate".[05] If the purpose of this area were also to teach, the arrangement of the amphitheatre and various other surrounding monuments appears to show that this was done on a large scale.

The arrangements shown in this part do not prove that the people of the Stone Ages knew about the heavens nor the size of the world. However, the monuments appear to be arranged to allow large scale teaching of how to prove what the world is, how to find its size and how to understand the heavens.

It is not possible to say what these monuments were really for. Nevertheless, the claim that Neolithic peoples did not have access to materials good enough to find out about their Universe is demonstrably wrong. If Stonehenge represents their knowledge, other monuments do exist in the location, setting, arrangement and type which would have allowed them the best opportunity to prove it.

4: FOLKLORE

If Stonehenge were used to explain the Universe, would there be evidence in folklore of such a dramatic event?

This chapter looks through some of the other mythological evidence and coincidences.

The Grail

Providing the dimensions are very similar or identical to those at Stonehenge, the invention described can produce a very bright 'mini-sun' to demonstrate a geocentric world's scientific principles. Regardless of the season, the 'mini-sun' appears at about the same height if a seasonal adjustment device is used (the 'three season device').

The castle-like structure of Stonehenge appears to be an ideal foundation arrangement for such a task: It is constructed of hard material which will not deflect much and can survive the occasional mishap when moving large poles or heavy mirror-laden timber frames.

The process of making a bright 'mini-sun' requires some additional components to be brought in procession to the inside of the castle-like round support structure.

The extra parts required are:

- A tree-pole or giant lance, pointed to the North Star;
- A hanger; rather like a candelabra because it carries a light and has a cross-bar which can be rotated;
- A cup shaped reflector, possibly containing crystals;
- A silvery dish composed of arrays of polished flat metal.

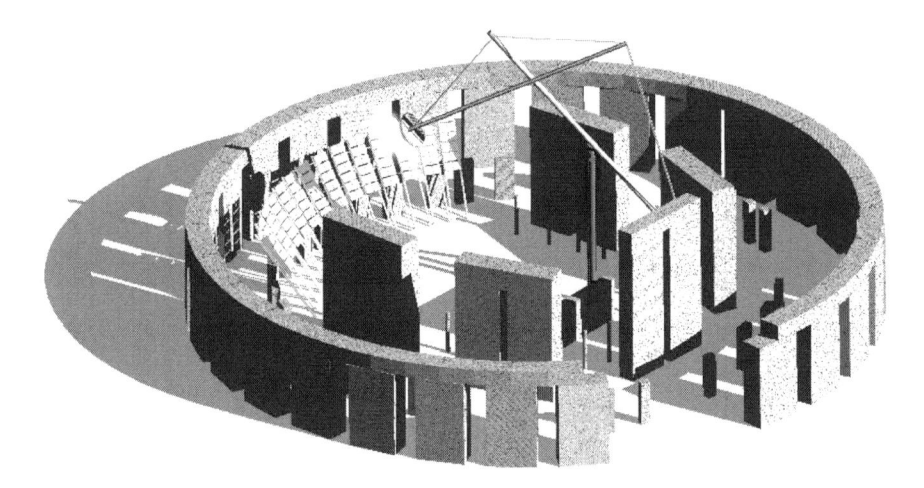

In the legend of the Arthurian Grail Procession, the grail is accompanied by several other objects brought into the Fisher King's castle. Perceval could have restored the Fisher King, but kept his silence and did not ask the question: "Unto whom one serveth the grail?". When Perceval awoke the next morning, the castle was empty.

At the castle, Perceval sees a strange procession passing by: A squire with a white lance, from which a drop of blood falls on his hand; two squires bearing candelabra; a noble maiden carrying a graal, a receptacle set with precious gems and shedding a brilliant light; another maiden with a platter of silver.

In the original version,[01] Chrétien did not write about the grail as if it were a religious object; only the later writers call it the "Holy Grail".

"...Qui une blance lance tint, Enpoingnie par emmi leu; Si passa par entre le feu....Pour çou ne le demanda mie. Atant dui varlet à lui vinrent, Qui candelers en lor mains tinrent De fin or ouvret à chisiel....Un graal entre ses ii- mains Une damoisièle tenoit.... Atout le graal qu'ele tint, Une si grans clartés i vint Que si pierdirent les candoiles Lor clarté, com font les estoiles Quant li solaus liëye ou la lune.... Piëres pressieuses avoit....Et li sire au varlet commande.. Qui tint le talléoir d'argent...."

If a reflector is used with the solar device described earlier in this text, the air around the 'great eye' of the reflector becomes hazy due to the concentrated sunlight. The 'candelabra' pole constantly rotates to follow the sun; so the bright reflector would seem to be covered by haze and would appear to move with sunbeams, fading as they fade.

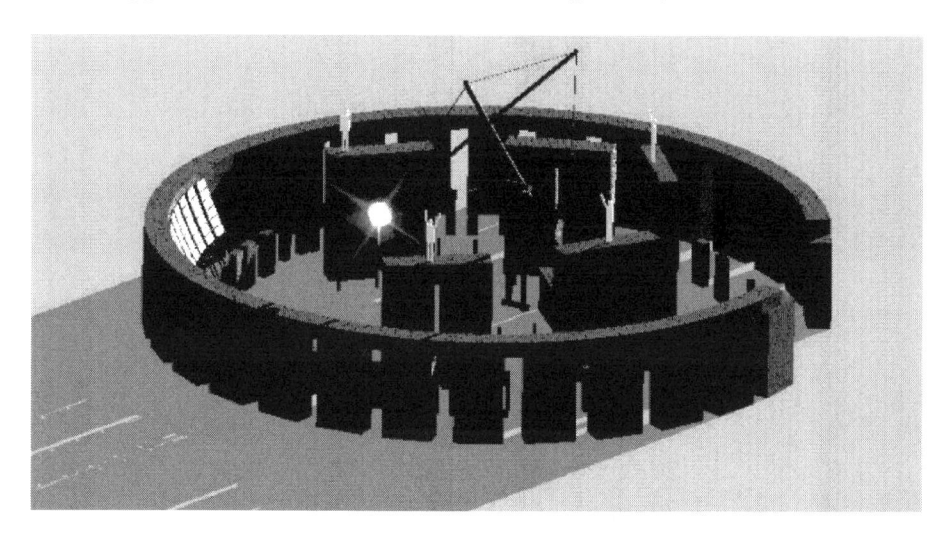

In the book 'Celtic Myth and Arthurian Romance',[02] the Grail's entry to Camelot is also described as if it were a solar concentrator:

> "It is Pentecost and Arthur and the knights of the round table are at Camelot. Every seat is full and because of this fulfilment Arthur states that *"it is the hour of the Glory of Lorges (England)"*. Even as Arthur speaks there blew a great wind about the castle and a mighty crash of thunder shook the place, then on a sudden a sunbeam cut through the gloom from end to end of the great hall, seven times more clear than ever man saw on the brightest day of summer ... Then the Holy Grail entered into the hall covered in a cloth of white samite, so filled with glorious light that none might behold it. Nor could they see who carried the Holy Grail, for it seemed to glide upon the sunbeam ... then on a sudden it departed from amongst them, and none might see where it went: but the sunbeam faded also."

Curiously, all of the components of the Grail Procession are the same as required to make Stonehenge into a solar concentrator. Chrétien's description of the Grail also happens to fit a description of this particular type of geocentric solar concentrator.

Treasures of the Tuatha Dé Danann

The Tuatha Dé Danann were a mythical race of Ireland who replaced the people known as the 'Fir Bog'. They were thought to have been in Ireland at about the same time that Stonehenge was in use. They are thought to have left Ireland at about the same time that Stonehenge fell into disuse (1500 BC).

The process of making a bright 'mini-sun' requires some additional components to be brought in procession to the inside of a castle-like round support structure:

- A tree-pole or giant lance, pointed to the North Star;
- A hanger and cup shaped reflector;
- A silvery dish composed of arrays of polished flat metal;
- A stone structure, such as at Stonehenge.

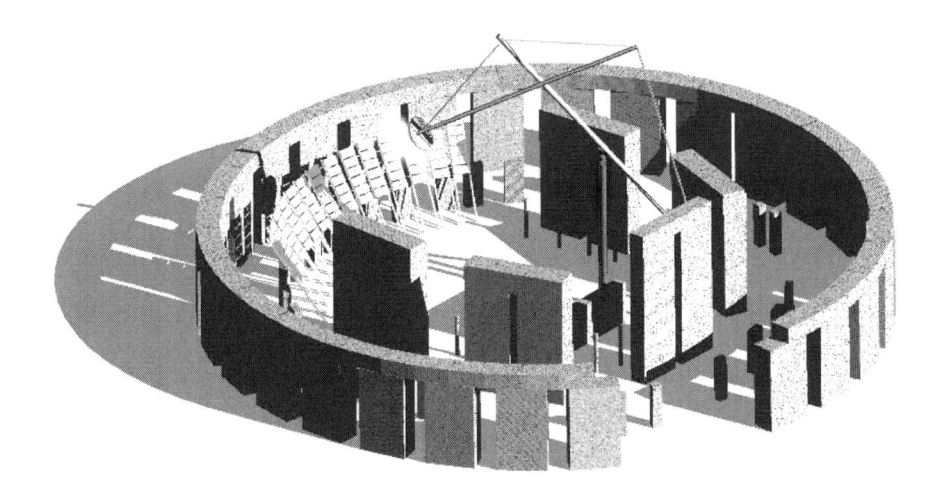

The Four Treasures of the Tuatha Dé Danann were:

- The Spear of Lug;
- The Sword of Light;
- The Cauldron of the Dagda;
- The Stone of Fál.

These four treasures could also describe Stonehenge, were it to be used to demonstrate a geocentric Universe.

The Druids

The druids of the Isles of Britain have passed down little or nothing of their tradition. Much of what is known of them comes from writings of Greek and Roman scholars. Of what is known, the records seem to agree that Druidry originated in Britain, the primary teaching was reincarnation, and that the Druids claimed to know the size of the world and movements of the heavens. A few samples are:

> "They have, however, their own kind of eloquence, and teachers of wisdom called Druids. They profess to know the size and shape of the world, the movements of the heavens and of the stars, and the will of the gods."
> Pomponius Mela, "De Situ Orbis", iii, 2, 18 and 19

> "They likewise discuss and impart to the youth many things respecting the stars and their motion, respecting the extent of the world and of our earth, respecting the nature of things, respecting the power and the majesty of the immortal gods"
> Cæsar, C. J., "De Bello Gallico", vi, 14 (MIT translation)

> "This institution {Druidry} is supposed to have been devised in Britain, and to have been brought over from it into Gaul; and now those who desire to gain a more accurate knowledge of that system generally proceed thither for the purpose of studying it."
> Cæsar, C. J., "De Bello Gallico", vi, 13 (MIT translation0

> "for the belief of Pythagoras prevails among them, that the souls of men are immortal and that after a prescribed number of years

they commence upon a new life, the soul entering into another body."
   Diodorus Siculus, "Library of History", v, 28:(Loeb/Thayer)

"At the present day, Britannia is still fascinated by magic, and performs its rites with so much ceremony that it almost seems as though it was she who had imparted the cult to the Persians. To such a degree do peoples throughout the whole world, although unlike and quite unknown to one another, agree upon this one point."
   Pliny, "Nat. Hist.", XXX, 13: (Thayer)

These descriptions appear to describe a people who had once solved the magic and mystery of the Hinge of the Heavens.

Summary

Stonehenge appears to be laid out as a geocentric description of the world. Its inner monument appears to be arranged as a geocentric demonstrator to create a ball of light rising above a round table which represents the world.

 Stonehenge's plan layout can be shown to be the same as an idealised geocentric description of the Universe. Its inner stone monument is demonstrated to be capable of producing a spectacular public display of solar movement.

The demonstrator's components appear to be the same as those described by Chrétien de Troyes when writing original stories about the Grail Procession. Descriptions of the grail also appear to be the same as a description of the device.

 The demonstrator's components also appear to be very similar to the Four Treasures of the Tuatha Dé Danann; a magical people of Ireland's past who, according to likely dates, lived in Ireland at about the same time as Stonehenge was in use.

 Descriptions of the Druids seem to tell of a people who had solved the mystery of the Hinge of the Heavens.

5: THE UNIVERSE

A geocentric universe describes a fixed world around which everything else rotates. In Ancient Greece, 6th century BC, Anaximander of Miletus first proposed that the Earth was a cylinder located at the centre of the Universe,[01] with everything else in the sky being holes set in invisible wheels which surround the Earth. The next big step was put forward by Ptolemy who, in the first century AD, proposed a mathematical scheme, with a spherical Earth at its centre, which could successfully predict the movement of planets.[02]

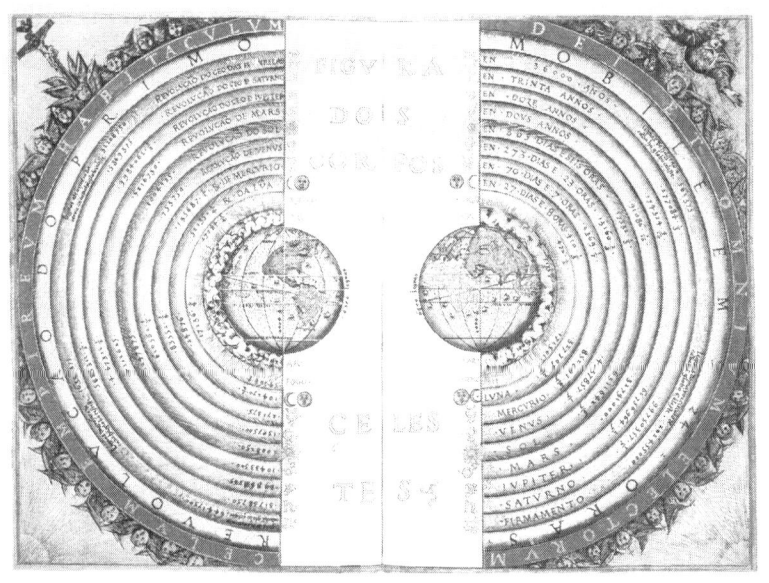

The Ptolemaic geocentric model of the Universe in 1568 Bartolomeu Velho (Bibliothèque Nationale de France, Paris). [03]

However, there were different views: Aristarchus of Samos, who lived nearly three hundred years before Ptolemy, had proposed that the Earth revolved about the Sun.[04] But long before Aristarchus, a follower of Pythagorus (named Philolaus) believed that the Earth revolved around a central fire.[05] This heliocentric theory was given short shrift by Aristotle, the leading philosopher of his day.[06]

Fifteen hundred years after Ptolemy, Copernicus re-introduced the idea that the Earth revolved around the Sun.

The Copernican system by Andreas Cellarius from the Harmonia Macrocosmica (1660) [07]

Copernicus' work was first printed in 1543, but the geocentric view persisted for a very long time; largely because his 'De revolutionibus orbium coelestium' (In English: On the Revolutions of the Heavenly Spheres) was considered incompatible with the Catholic faith. It was therefore listed by decree, in 1616, on the 'Index of Forbidden Books'.

Coincidences: Part 1

In 1559, William Cuningham, in his book 'The Cosmographical Glasse', drew out the established view; showing how the sun seems to rotate about a fixed world. In the image below, his original drawing has been faded (on the right hand side) to allow the solstice positions to be seen:

A geocentric view: Extract from 'The Cosmographical Glasse' of 1559 [08]

Cuningham has chosen to view the world looking towards the east. This eastwards view allowed him to show both the angle of the polar axis and also how the zodiacal constellations (from the tropic of Cancer to Capricorn) intersect with the solar planes at the solstices.

Similarly, Stonehenge is built in a perfect circle and has a circular bank outside. The axis to the Heel-stone, along the Avenue, is in the correct direction to show the polar axis (just *over* 51° clockwise from north). Stonehenge has four markers known as the Station Stones; which are also in the correct position to show the position of the sun at its extremes: The two solstices.

Cuningham has shown thirty six markers; one for every ten degrees. But other marker systems are possible: Stonehenge is one seventh of a world's diameter from the equator. Fifty six divides into seven precisely, leaving seven sub-division points between each marker. Within Stonehenge's bank, there are fifty six markers known as Aubrey holes.

Stonehenge's circular bank is unusual[09] in that it has a ditch *outside* the bank. By comparison, most other 'henges', such as Avebury, have an arrangement which has a ditch inside the bank. This inwardly facing bank at Stonehenge could represent the outer edge of the Universe.

Stonehenge is at a latitude of 51°10'44"; almost precisely one seventh of the way around the world from the equator. If a line representing the equator were drawn onto Stonehenge's plan, its Station Stones are at an angle of approximately 24° relative to that 'equator'. In 2500 BC, the sun's apparent movement was 24° either side of the equator:

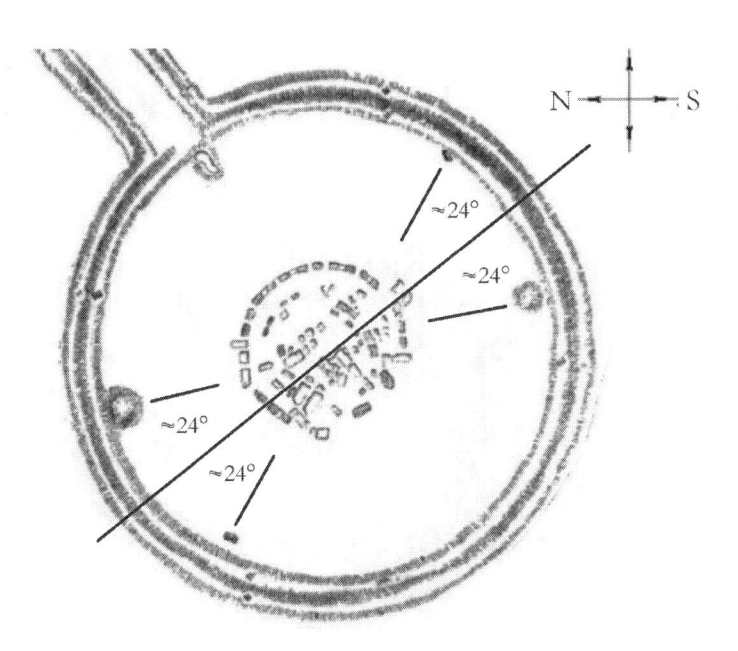

Modified & updated version of Stonehenge 1845 Ground plan

Using fifty-six degrees of measurement rather than the modern equivalent (360°), each solstice stone marker must be 3.7 of the fifty-six 'degree posts' away from the equator line (i.e. 24°×56/360°). At Stonehenge, stone 91 is approximately 3.7 Aubrey holes away from hole 14. Stone 93 is approximately 3.4 holes from hole 42. Stones 92 and 94, though both now missing, were about 3.7 holes away from holes 14 and 42 respectively.

Coincidences: Part 2

The earlier coincidences within this chapter establish that there may be some sort of existing ('a priori') evidence for a geocentric connection. Stonehenge also has an internal structure, as described earlier, which precisely duplicates a system designed to show and explain the geocentric nature of the Universe.

To re-cap, the similarities related to the internal structure are listed below. Explanations and diagrams of detailed mathematics and engineering considerations have been shown in the notes rather than in the main text:

<u>1: Height of winter mirror rim</u>
The base of the winter polar axis rod must be set at ground level,[11] it must be accessible and people must be able to see the 'shining star' from outside.[12-14] Either by trial and error, or by design, there is only one really good way to make this work.[15&16] And for a 32m diameter bowl, this arrangement sets the height of the outside edge at a maximum of 5.0m tall (16'5").[17]
- Stonehenge's outer sarsen ring has a height of about 4.9m to the top of its outer rim (Stones 1–30). It also has an external diameter of about 32m. However, there is nothing particularly special about this coincidence, because we started with the assumption that this is what we might be looking at: So this coincidence is just a starting point.

<u>2: Diameter of circular rim for the winter arrangement</u>
Because a 32m (105') diameter mirror sphere sits above the circular rim, the internal diameter should be slightly smaller. The smallest diameter, for this size, which fits at this latitude is just under 30m (≈99').[18]
- Stonehenge's internal diameter is just under 30m.

<u>3: Pure circular rim, internally facing for the winter arrangement</u>
The lintels need sufficient depth to allow placement of the winter mirrors. They would also need to be circular on their internal faces so that the mirror frames can be placed in the correct initial position.
- Stonehenge has a pure circular rim, internally facing.

4: Level surface at top of outer lintels

To make this work easily, the mirror frames need to be positioned so that their tops are level. For the winter position, if frames are made to lean against a circular rim, they can be set to the correct height using a fixed distance (up or down) from some sort of level surface: The mirrors have now become part of a sphere, but still need final focusing.

- Stonehenge's outer lintel stones form a precise circle with a level top surface.

5: Flat surfaces of supports

The external pillars, arranged in a circle, would require a flat internal face to allow positioning of the bottom of the mirror frames: Using a fixed length rod, these can then be quickly set to position and the bottom ends raised if required. Once done, the mirrors are almost perfectly focused.

- At Stonehenge, the external sarsens (Stones 1–30) are flat-faced on the inward-facing surface.

6: The dimensions of the sphere and the polar axis socket

At a 16m (52' 6") mirror sphere radius, the bottom of the winter pole will be located at ground level provided the centre of hinge (and the mirror sphere) is just under 10m (≈33") above ground level. This means that the back face of the socket must be both directly south of the centre and located about 8m (≈26') away from the centre (see note 13).

- At Stonehenge, a socket occurs at the easterly edge of Stone 54. The easterly edge of Stone 54 is directly south of the centre of Stonehenge. The back of the socket is within six inches (15cm) of the circle's centre line, going in a north-south direction, and is located approximately 8m (≈26') away from the centre of the monument.

7: Detailed dimensions of the lowest socket

The lowest socket should be oriented towards the centre (looking north) and should also point upwards. This allows a tree-pole to be brought in and then raised up to an angle of 51°.

- At Stonehenge, the lowermost socket on Stone 54 is oriented to the north and, although badly damaged, is arranged as a curious egg-shaped socket whose top surface tapers away. This would allow a tree-pole to be brought in and then raised to angle of about 51°.

8: Platform Stones set to correct plane and location for access

Although spherical solar concentration works by focusing to a line to get concentrated light (see Appendix B), the best length for the rotating rod will be between 8m-10m (≈26'-33') for a 16m (≈52') radius mirror sphere. To allow access to the end of this focal point (on the rod), a good solution is to use thin platforms which cast the least shadow.

- At Stonehenge, a thin horse-shoe shape has been installed with four sets of short trilithons (stones 51&52, 53&54, 57&58, and 59&60). Each stone set, including the Great Trilithon (55&56), is set at a height which allows access to the end of the rod for each of the three levels (see 11 below for explanation and notes on the 'three-season' levels).

9: Trilithons set to correct locations for hauling

To make an effective hinge, some sort of platform arrangement is also needed against which the sail can be rotated (around the tree-pole) using ropes. These platforms must not cast too much shadow on the mirrors at any time of year. For this reason, any hauling platforms near the mirrors should be the shortest.

- Stonehenge has five sets of internal trilithons (Stones 51&52, 53&54, 55&56, 57&58 and 59&60). In addition to appearing to be configured for access, these sets also double-up as hauling platforms and appear to be ideally configured for it (see tests done in Appendix B). They are also arranged so that they cast the least shadow: The shortest trilithon pairs (51&52 and 59&60) are at the front.

10: The Great Trilithon

Stones 55 and 56 (the Great Trilithon) are 7.5m tall. However, if Stonehenge were a geocentric concentrator, the current position of the remaining Great Trilithon stone would be better sited half a metre or so towards the north east.

- Recently, it has been discovered that this trilithon stone was re-positioned by the Victorians: It was moved from the north east.

11: The upper sockets

As the sun's plane goes up with the approach of summer, the plane of the focal circle (of the equipment) goes down. To adjust for this, the rotating rod must be tilted downwards. To get the focal point to stay at approximately the same height above the lintels throughout the year, the equipment must be raised so that the rotator can be hauled from the same set of platforms: This happens once for equinox and again for summer. The mirrors can be tilted and re-positioned (see also 13 below).

The solar plane varies with a sinusoidal motion, which means that the position of the solar plane is in the bottom 15% of the range in winter, then from 15% to 85% during spring, and the top 15% in summer. If the equipment were raised, the ideal[19] vertical distance between the top and the bottom polar socket will be about 4.2m (13'9').

- At Stonehenge, there appear to be two further sockets on the edge of Stone 54. These are in a vertical line within that one stone. The dimension from the lowest to the top socket is about 4.2m (13'9'). Although the sockets appear damaged, perhaps from centuries of use, each of these sockets appears to be correctly orientated to receive a tree-pole placed at an angle of 51°.

Measuring at Stonehenge

12: Special (unusual) packing for the 'Socket stone'

This stone, being the only stone which is required to have tree-poles raised against it, needs to have special foundations.

- Stonehenge's Stone 54 has unique packing, is the heaviest stone of all at Stonehenge, and has an unusual bulbous footing. This stone is also the correct size to accept the huge lateral forces generated by raising a tree-pole.[20]

13: Spring & autumn mirror supports: Height

The secondary mirror supports have to be arranged in a circle, particularly about the north east. These support stones must also be the correct height and location: This positioning all depends on the location of the centre of the hinge when the tree-pole is placed in the second socket.

For the spherical demonstrator, with an internal diameter of some 30m (≈100'), a secondary support ring at the north east, approximately 23m to 24m (75' - 79') in its plan diameter and some 2m (6'6") high, would suit the task (see illustration in notes).[21] Note that other diameters are possible providing the height of support is modified to suit.

- At Stonehenge, the north east blue stones are arranged in a circular arc approximately 23.5m (77') in diameter *and* about 2m (6'6") in height.

Support stones for the equinox positions carry mirror frames and would therefore need to be strong. Location and setting can be done using fixed lengths measured from the larger finished stones of the outer rim, so these stones would need only a rough finish.

- Cleal et al. describe in detail how the Bluestone Circle stones, that is the circle of upright 'bluestones' just within the outer 'walls' of Stonehenge, are heavy and roughly made compared with the innermost bluestone horse-shoe.

14: Smooth faces on shorter Platform Stones

The shorter platform stones (including the 'Socket stone') would ideally be smooth internally (especially to prevent jarring as the sail is raised). From the tests done in 2013 (see Appendix B), we discovered that smooth faces also make an ideal back reflector which can be used to precisely focus mirrors once they are placed in their initial position.

- At Stonehenge, all of the Trilithons have smooth internal faces. However, the Great Trilithon has a smoother surface on the outside face.

15: Early configurations

The Q&R holes at Stonehenge appear to be in the correct position for a slightly smaller structure designed to do exactly the same thing as the late structure. There is also evidence that some of the bluestones were originally lintels (see Chapter 1:'The Stones: A potted summary'.)

16: Internal timer ring (inner horse-shoe) in correct location
If a plumb bob at the back end of the sail is dropped to a set of markers, the position of the sail can be judged with time. This might be important on a day which might prove cloudy. If this existed, an elliptical or semi-elliptical ring of stones would be an ideal arrangement; and this ring of markers could only be constructed within the larger trilithon horse-shoe.
• The bluestones of Stonehenge's inner horse-shoe are (by comparison with the bluestones near the external rim) well tooled, polished, elegantly composed, shaped and neatly arranged. They are also in good positions to act as a timing ring (see illustration in notes).[22]

17: Instructions on how to put up the pole and sail
To make it absolutely clear to anyone setting up the pole, a drawing of the sail and pole might be carved into the side of the 'Socket stone'.
• At Stonehenge, at the edge of Stone 54 (the stone with the sockets), there is a T-shaped relief carving. It is known as the 'Chief's Face' because it looks a little like a representation of eyebrows and a very long nose. The 'T' also has the correct relative dimensions to show the pole, its sail and the counterbalance distance necessary.[23]

Stone 54 (photo courtesy of Terence Meaden)

18: T shapes
At Stonehenge, other large T shapes appear to exist on the back of 53, 54 and the side of 53. From recent scans, large numbers of additional T shapes also exist on the front face of stone 53 (see Chapter 1:'New Evidence'.)

19: Location
On a geocentric world, drawn to show the axis of the North Pole at Stonehenge's location, the position of Stonehenge itself is at the top of that image of the world: This position is directly east of the centre (see also illustration in notes). [24]

- From recent laser scans, almost all remaining T shapes cut into the stones are on those stones directly east of centre.

20: Viewing
The arrangement would ideally be viewed from the best possible angle: For a concentrator designed to be seen in the afternoon, with the morning used to set the arrangement up (and check that it all works), this direction is from the north east along a long strip of ground.

- At Stonehenge, recent laser scanning has revealed that the monument was specifically designed to be seen from the north east. The Avenue, a wide strip of land coming from the north east, would have been ideal for viewing.

21: Metals
A large amount of archaeological evidence backs up the idea that metals were in use at Stonehenge before it was built. If mirrors were in use, they would have been exceptionally valuable, so unlikely to be lost. Nevertheless, a tablet of tin was found at Stonehenge with, on one side, an inscription in a lost and unknown language (see Chapter 1; 'Metals and Stonehenge'.)

22: Legend
If such a thing were done, there would be expected to be legends passed down through generations. In the case of a solar concentrator, several of those legends appear to exactly describe what was done (see Chapter 4).

23: Remains of knowledge
If the meaning of the heavens were known at Stonehenge, there might be expected to be the remains of experiments showing how this was known: There do appear to be large numbers of such remains, all configured as required, along the South Coast of England (see Chapter 3.)

24: The meaning of Heel
The word heel is derived from the meaning 'to rotate'. The word 'Yule', meaning the time of winter solstice, is also thought to derive from this word. [25]

- At Stonehenge, the stone with this name is the same as the stone about which the Universe rotates. (for more see Chapter 1; 'Potted history: Stage 2'.)

25: The meaning of Stonehenge
The words Stone and Henge are remarkably similar to all North European words for stone, hinge, tin and angle: These words happen to describe the main features of the solar concentrator mechanism (see Chapter 1:'Stonehenge: The word'.)

In short, there is nothing about Stonehenge which suggests that it was not capable of demonstrating the nature of the Neolithic Universe.

Summary

The coincidences described in the first two parts may just be coincidences. Nevertheless, they describe every single aspect of the design at Stonehenge.

The British Isles have long been fascinated with magic. Authors such as Tolkien and Rowling have brought new life to old folklore.

Tales of magical wands, shields, bright lights and mysterious powers are all recorded in British and Irish legend. Getting tin and other metals from stone, a process which requires a stream or lake, would have been the first step in the magical process of making a mirror.

When Leonardo da Vinci produced the Last Supper, one of the most reproduced religious painting of all time, it is said that people would watch the drawing for hours. The painting used the new idea of perspective to focus on the central figure and also showed 'real person' reactions of the disciples:

The Last Supper (public domain version)

This was the reaction of people familiar with the new sciences of the 16th century.

But the people of the Neolithic had only just started to imagine science: A bright daytime 'mini-sun' created on Earth would have had an immense impact on how they saw their place in the world.

Stonehenge's plan layout is the same as an idealised geocentric description of the Universe. Its inner stone monument is capable of producing a spectacular public display of solar movement. The arrangement of this system appears to be based on a simple method of tracking celestial objects.

Perhaps Stonehenge was a depository of knowledge about the Universe. A place of learning, it could also have been the primary source of Arthurian stories of magic and its power. Some legends of magic perhaps remain only as fragments of the Old World's knowledge?

Greek legend tells of a Titan named Hyperion: [26]

> *"Of Hyperion we are told that he was the first to understand, by diligent attention and observation, the movement of both the sun and the moon and the other stars, and the seasons as well, in that they are caused by these bodies, and to make these facts known to others; and that for this reason he was called the father of these bodies, since he had begotten, so to speak, the speculation about them and their nature."*

And of a mysterious people known as the Hyperboreans who lived in the north on a very large island somewhere beyond the Mediterranean: [27]

> *"There lies in the Ocean an island no smaller than Sicily. This island, the account continues, is situated in the north and is inhabited by the Hyperboreans, who are called by that name because their home is beyond the point whence the north wind (Boreas) blows ... And there is also on the island both a magnificent sacred precinct of Apollo and a notable temple which is adorned with many votive offerings and is spherical in shape ... The account is also given that the god visits the island every nineteen years, the period in which the return of the stars to the same place in the heavens is accomplished."*

If England was Hyperborea, and Hyperion also represents those people, then Stonehenge's lost purpose, to store and save ancient North European knowledge about the nature of our Universe, was only rediscovered by the Ancient Greeks thousands of years later.

6: EPILOGUE

If the stone monument was a geocentric description of the Universe, it specifically focuses on the movement of the sun at its solstices more than any other astronomical feature.

Evidence suggests that the original monument, before the stones were placed, was originally aligned to solstice. Some say that this was the sunset at mid-winter (approx December 21) whereas others say it was the dawn at mid-summer (approx June 21). Yet others claim it was both: At Stonehenge, these two directions are almost exactly the opposite of each other.

At the time in which the first phase of the original monument was constructed, huge swathes of land were being set aside for the construction of two cursuses. These two pieces of land point towards times of year which are either side of equinox (either 20 March or 22 September). Of the two, the Great Cursus is nearer to the equinox 'alignment'. At some point before Stonehenge was built, these cursuses were abandoned.

Some believe that Stonehenge, the new monument of stone, enhanced the solstice alignment in some way. But, if you agree with this book, you may also agree that it probably does not.

Whatever the reason for the early solstice connection, the motivation to construct the stones is likely to be connected to whatever had happened in the times long before. If Stonehenge was all about knowledge, any explanation for what happened before must be profoundly simple, logical and obvious: And it will explain why Stonehenge had to be built, regardless of the cost.

Many people believe that Stonehenge was a temple devoted to the worship of the sun. Was worship of the Sun involved? I am not so sure: Though the Sun was obviously very important to the people, there is other evidence, near Stonehenge and elsewhere, that something else had been going on: Something older, and more important to them, than honouring a God named Apollo.

The Universe described by Stonehenge would dispel the fears of the old times. Some of those ideas would be set in stone to become a permanent reminder of the triumph of the new beliefs. As time went by, the new would become an unquestionable doctrine.

But although Stonehenge may have overthrown the old fears, they would remain sulking, but still tended, at more ancient places far away. And Stonehenge, as mighty and as permanent as it was, would never fully dispel the old ways: Eventually, they would re-emerge, reinvigorated with a newly discovered set of certainties; stronger than those of Stonehenge itself. Stonehenge's permanence, and its reassuring self-belief, may have been a cause of the downfall of the civilisation that built it.

Thousands of years ago, people feasted at the time of Yule. They may have exchanged presents. Over the winter solstice, they may have celebrated their beliefs by congregating around a tree-pole which became filled with light.

Thousands of years later, people feast at the time of Yule. They exchange presents. During the time of the winter solstice, some celebrate by congregating around a tree filled with light. But the old fears, which seem to be described in some ancient places, have re-emerged in a new but familiar form.

APPENDIX A: The rotation of our planet

The Earth rotates a full turn every day, which gives the appearance that the Moon and the Sun go around us.

Our planet also moves in a big circle around the Sun, but our North Pole always points to the North Star: This star is at right angles to our direction (or plane) of spin, but is not at right angles to our orbit around the Sun.

3,000 years ago, the 'Guardians of the (North) Pole' were the stars Kochab and Pherkab. Polaris, known to the Greeks as Phoenice, was just an ordinary star at the other end of the Big Dipper.

Every 26,000 years or so the celestial pole turns in a full circle with a radius of some 23.4°. Alrai (Gamma Cepheii) will become the Pole Star in a thousand years followed by Alderamin (Alpha Cephei) in 7500AD. The role passes to Deneb, Alpha Cygnis, in 9000AD and then Vega, opposite to Polaris, in 14000AD.[01] Our planet, like most others, 'tumbles' in space so slowly that we have the same pole star from year to year.

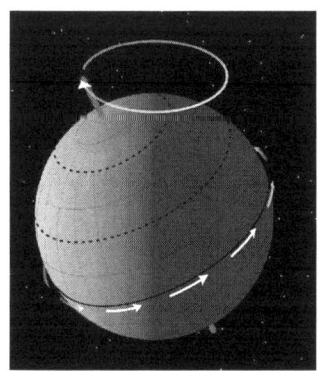

Precession: Image courtesy of NASA

Our planet rotates about the current celestial polar axis once a day. Every 365 days or so, we also orbit the Sun in a squashed circle known as the Elliptic. Our orbit also has its own polar axis, which is 23° or so away from the Earth's celestial polar axis. Another term; the Ecliptic, describes the apparent path of the Sun around our world. To avoid confusion, this book refers to this as 'the solar plane'.

Night and day are caused by the daily rotation of the World about its polar axis. Winter happens, in the Northern Hemisphere, when the North Pole faces away from the sun (by the 'tilt' of 23.5°). Six months later, around the other side of our orbit, the North pole faces towards the sun giving the Northern Hemisphere its summer:

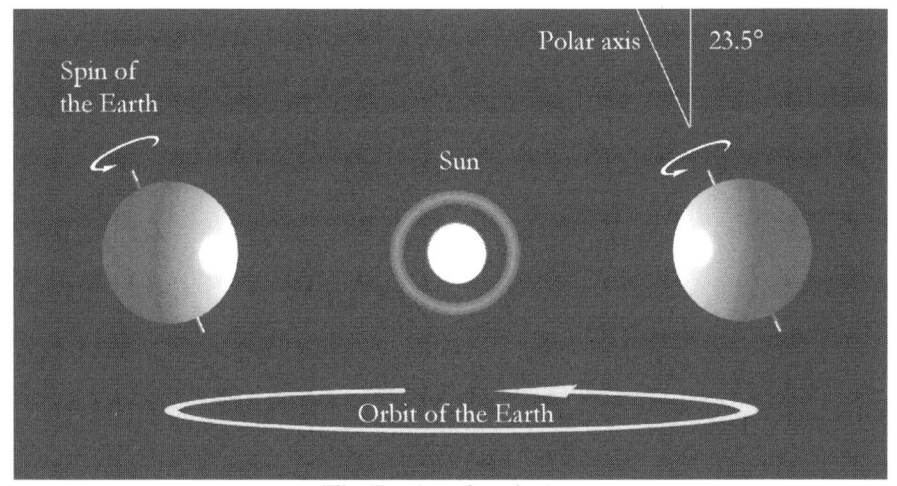

The Earth circling the Sun

Our 'tilt' is currently 23.5° away from the plane of our orbit. However, even this changes over time: Over the last million years or so, it has varied between 22° 02' 33" and 24° 30' 16", with a mean period of 41,040 years. [02] In 3000 BC, it was close to 24° rather than the 23.5° we have now.

Some technical stuff

At higher latitudes, we need heat most in the winter and least in the summer. Because the Earth is rotated away from the Sun in winter, its rays fall at a shallower angle; so fewer watts of energy hit each square metre of soil. In addition, the sun's rays must travel through a greater distance of atmosphere.

At the edge of the atmosphere, the sun's energy density is 1,412 W/m^2 in early January and some 1,321 W/m^2 in early July.[03] Our orbit brings us slightly closer to the sun in the winter resulting in the northern hemisphere facing away from the sun when it is at its 'warmest'. This effect gives the Northern Hemisphere slightly less extreme temperatures than the Southern Hemisphere.

The Sun, a yellow dwarf, emits heat and light (black body radiation) at around about the same wavelengths detected by our eyes. Of the radiation that hits our planet, the highest frequencies are largely absorbed by the outer atmosphere so that, at the top of mountains, the energy density rarely exceeds 1,100 W/m^2.

At ground level along the Equator, when the sun is directly overhead during the spring and autumn equinoxes, the midday solar energy density perpendicular to solar rays can reach 950-1,000 W/m^2.[04] At this time and location, the energy only travels through one atmosphere's 'worth' (known as an 'Air Mass'). At the start and the end of the day, the rays must travel through a greater distance; so a greater proportion is reflected or absorbed by the air.[05]

The further the light has to travel after striking the upper atmosphere, the more of the remaining ozone filtered light is reflected by air, dust and clouds. At the Equator, a greater proportion of the high energy radiation gets through; the sky is a darker hue of blue during the day than it is at higher latitudes. Clouds also reflect light and can drastically reduce the amount of radiation getting through.

However, clouds also deflect and re-reflect light: In addition to the direct brightness which causes shadows (known as 'In Beam' irradiation), some additional light will arrive due to scatter from molecules and Aerosols (dust, water, pollutant) within the atmosphere.

Apparent solar planes

Our celestial (polar) axis is currently at about 23.5° to the axis of our orbit around the sun, but five thousand years ago it was nearer to 24°. This resulted in the sun being higher in the summer and lower in the winter. Warmer summers, but colder winters.

If we consider the Earth as fixed and we stand at the equator to watch the Sun move over a year, the Sun would appear to have an odd orbit which spirals from north to south. If we recorded the daily position of the spiral over a year, we would notice that it has a sinusoidal pattern which lingers over the North and South Poles during the solstices. The spiral then passes fairly quickly overhead during the equinoxes of late March and late September.

We would also record that the Sun moves 23.5° to the north in June, back to zero at the equinox and then 23.5° to the south for December.

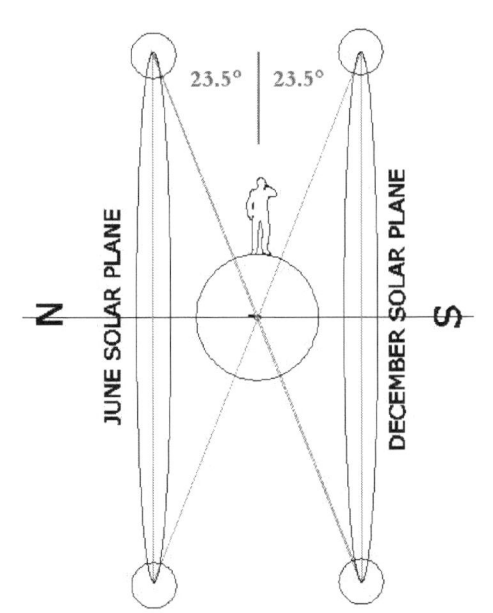

Movement of the Sun seen from the Equator

All of the above effects are a result of our celestial axis being rotated at 23.5° to the axis of rotation of our orbit around the sun. The daily movement along this spiral is in a nearly flat circle known as the Solar Plane (or Ecliptic).

APPENDIX A: The rotation of our planet

If we move to Northern Europe and again consider the world to be fixed, our solar plane instead moves overhead during the summer resulting in longer days. In the winter it appears to move south, resulting in shorter days.

As at the Equator, we also would observe that the annual movement is sinusoidal. This results in the sun spending longer periods of time at very shallow angles in winter and at very high angles (overhead) in summer. We also see relatively quick changes of this angle over the autumnal and spring Equinoxes.

The man in the picture below, at a northern latitude of about 51°, sees the 'equatorial sun' (during equinox) at an angle of 39° up from ground level (90°-51°). This gives a maximum sun angle of about 62.5° in summer (39°+23.5°) and results in short shadows. In winter he sees shallow solstice angles of up to about 15.5° (39°-23.5°), resulting in the long shadows of winter.

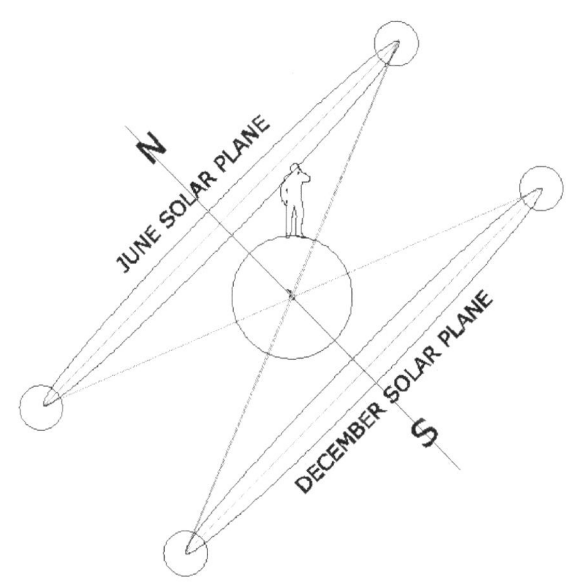

Solar Planes; movement of the Sun seen at temperate latitudes

Because we spin quickly around our polar axis every 24 hours, the apparent daily movement of the sun is a nearly flat circle, a little like to the wheels of a bicycle, with the spokes representing time. As we move around the sun, this circle, the 'solar plane', moves slowly up and down the polar axis.

STONEHENGE

In the picture below, the wheels represent the apparent path of the Sun around our planet, as seen from Stonehenge during winter and summer. If the wheels were turned to face south, an ant on the ball at the centre of the picture would see that the wheels have exactly the same path as the sun on the days of the two equinoxes:

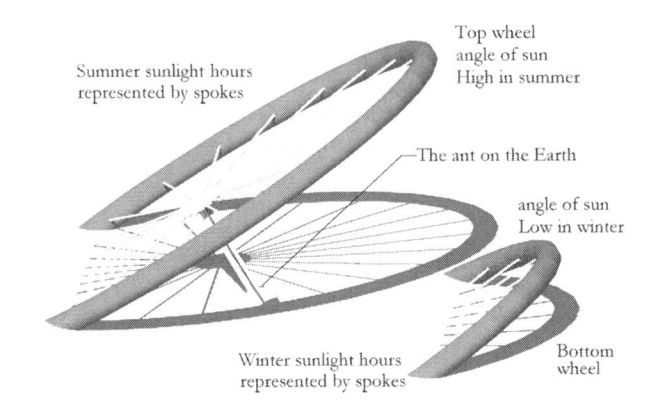

Information on how the sun's rays affect Britain has been catalogued and plotted by the Chartered Institution of Building Services Engineers, in their excellent 'Design Guide A':

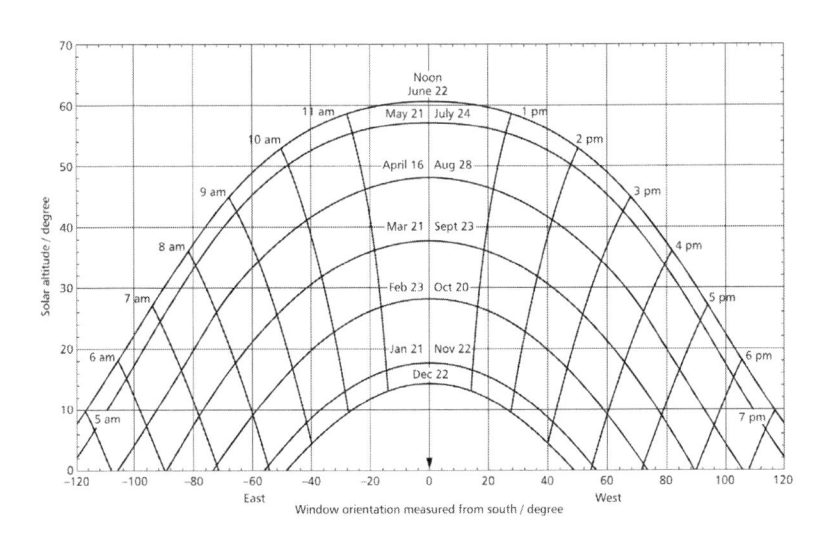

Solar Azimuths: Extract from CIBSE Design Guide A: Figure 2-12 (reproduced with permission)

APPENDIX B: Spherical solar collectors

If a set of mirrors are arranged as a sphere, rays of light are reflected from the mirrors in the way described in this book.

Spherical solar collectors, unlike parabolas, focus to a line rather than a point. However, a lot of the energy from the mirrors is focused to a point located at one half of the radius of the spherical mirror-bowl. The mirrors of a sphere only work as an effective parabola when they are within, or less than, thirty degrees of the source direction (i.e. sunbeams). If needed, all of the energy from a selected set of spherical mirrors can be made to focus to an effective point for periods of up to four hours.

On a daily basis, the mirrors need to remain fixed in position. This is particularly necessary if low-quality frames and materials are used. In summer, when the sun is high, the focus of the mirrors ends at a low circle going round a half-sphere. In winter, the focus is higher.

If mirrors were the most expensive thing in the world and spherical solar collection was the only known way to collect concentrated solar power, it would make sense to rearrange the mirrors to get the best efficiency. In this book, this method of arrangement is known as a 'three-season device'.

Background

Many decades go, other solutions using spherical solar collectors were proposed. Spherical mirrors, as opposed to parabolas, concentrate to a line parallel to the rays of the sun rather than a point. However, within certain ranges, the array approximates to a parabola and can focus to a point.

Several patents using this principle were taken out during the 1970s. These solar collectors use a fixed spherical mirror bowl which concentrates the light to a line which lies between 0.5 radii and the face of the bowl.

The idea was that the arrangement would pivot and also rotate so that it aligned to the direction of the sun. This arrangement has the advantage that the mirrors are fixed and therefore inexpensive to build.

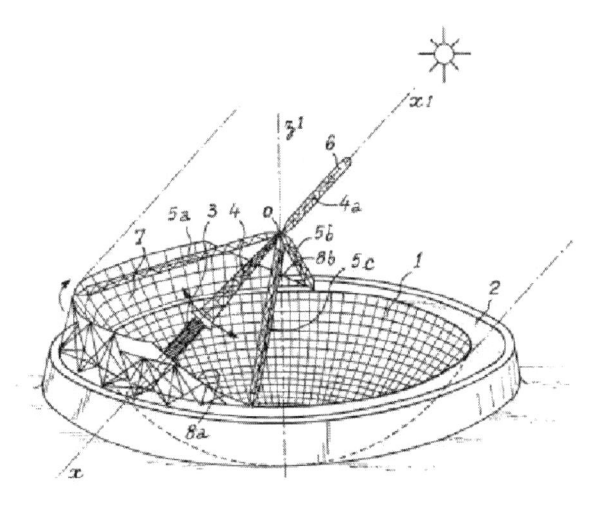

Extract from US patent no 4170985

A version of this idea had already been implemented at the Arecibo Observatory, near Arecibo, Puerto Rico. This was originally planned to be a parabolic dish until Ward Low of the Advanced Research Projects Agency noted that one other form of energy concentration could be fixed. The 'hemispherical bowl' concept, which resulted from the subsequent collaboration between Air Force Cambridge Research Laboratory and Professor William E. Gordon, allows the focus rather than the bowl to be moved to stay aligned with stellar objects.

APPENDIX B: Spherical solar collectors 115

Theory

Spherical solar collectors focus to a line. However, the distribution of intensity of ray radiation along the line is not constant: The rays tend to concentrate towards the centre of the bowl at the half radius point.

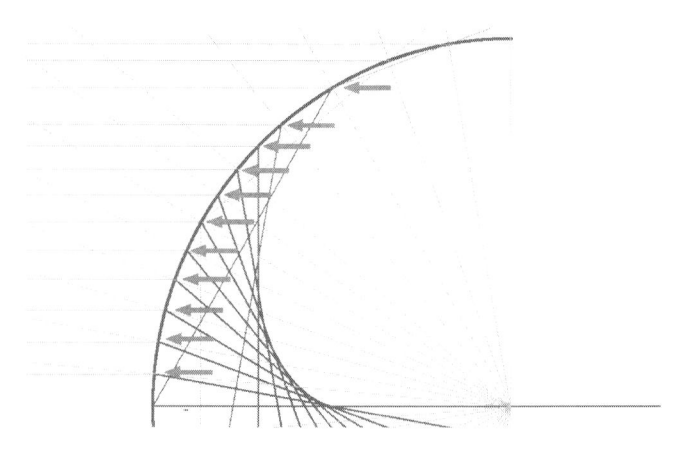

Ray reflection lines from a spherical mirror

For fixed mirror bowls with a moving solar object, only the central area of the bowl mimics a parabola. This central area continuously changes as the sun moves.

Zooming into the half radius focal point, a line can be off-set so that a greater number of rays can be collected (shown as positions A and position B below). At a strike angle of up to 30° or so on the mirrors, the incoming reflected light can be concentrated to a very small focus area.

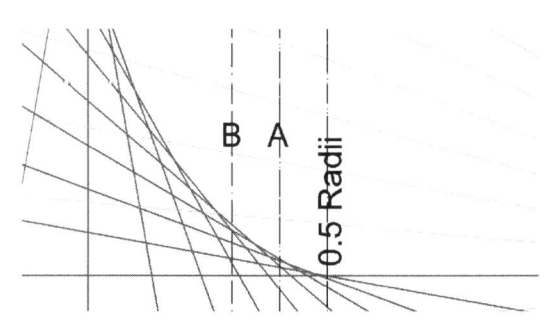

Zooming in to the half-radius point

In addition, if the reflector at the off-set is made larger than required, the sphere can be composed of flat square segments of mirror rather than a pure sphere.

The end of this focus (the half radius point) is effectively invertedly mirroring the path of the Sun around the Earth. During winter, the end point on the surface of the half radius focal sphere traces a high circular plane. The diameter of this plane circle slightly expands slightly during autumn (or spring) and then slightly contracts again during the summer.

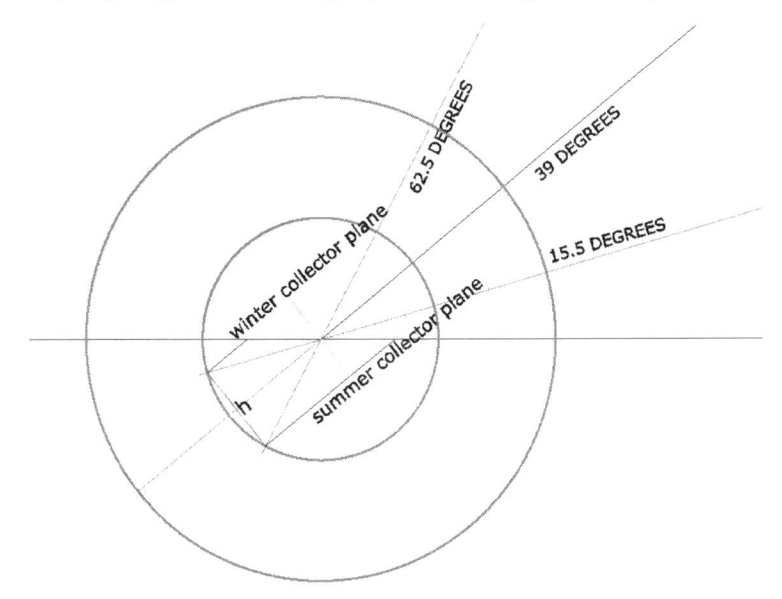

If the apparent orbit of the Sun were a pure circle, this movement (of the reflector focus point) will exactly mirror the Sun's path, showing how it moves if the Earth were thought to be at the centre of the Universe.

The above considerations show that a small flat plate, if moving in a circle and at a constant speed (similar to a 24 hour clock), will concentrate incoming light rays from a spherical mirror set.

If we decide that we are only going to collect the most productive light, the number of mirrors can be cut down to include only those mirrors that will provide concentrated light to the collector (or reflection plate). This seasonal range of daily movement translates to a 'slice' taken through the sphere of mirrors: So the most useful mirror arrangement would become a slice of a sphere produced by a moving 'eye'.

APPENDIX B: Spherical solar collectors 117

Consider the movement of the 'eye' as it turns in a circle: The collector will 'sweep' over the surface of the spherical mirrors as the sun moves around its daily solar plane:

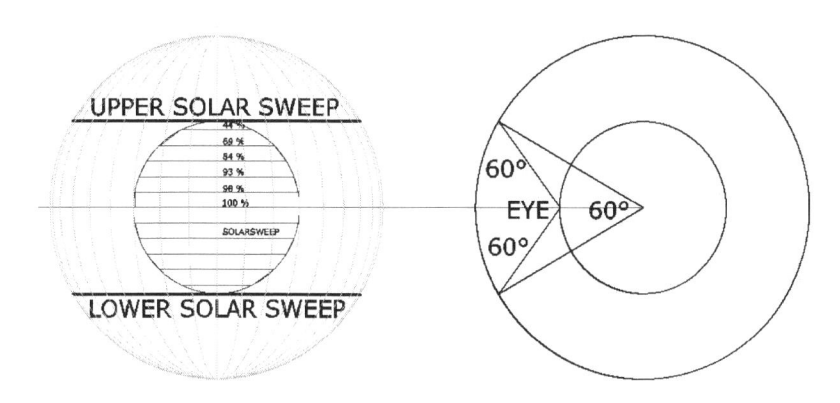

Equinoctial solar sweeps of spherical mirrors

If the axes are rotated to the winter and summer planes (23.5° either side of equinox), 'mirror bands' are obtained from which concentrated sunlight could be captured:

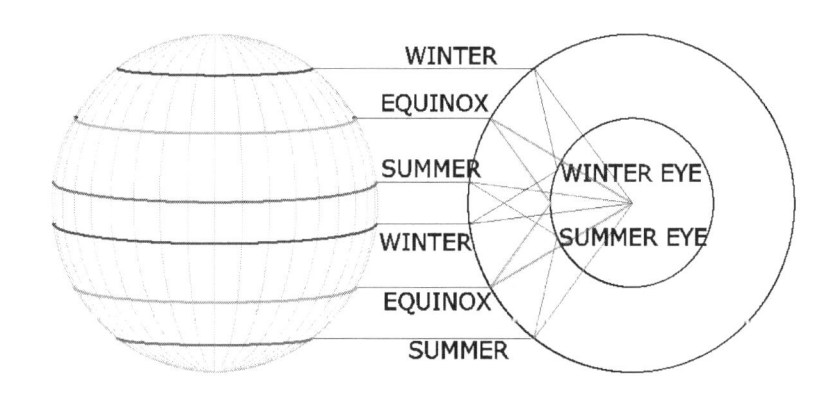

Seasonal solar sweeps

These bands now show the best position of mirrors if they are arranged to capture this light using spherical methods.

By rotating the arrangement to suit the latitude, the best mirror arrangement can be found for any chosen period of time. At high latitudes, we need heat most in the winter, so the ideal mirror-bowl would be at a steep angle:

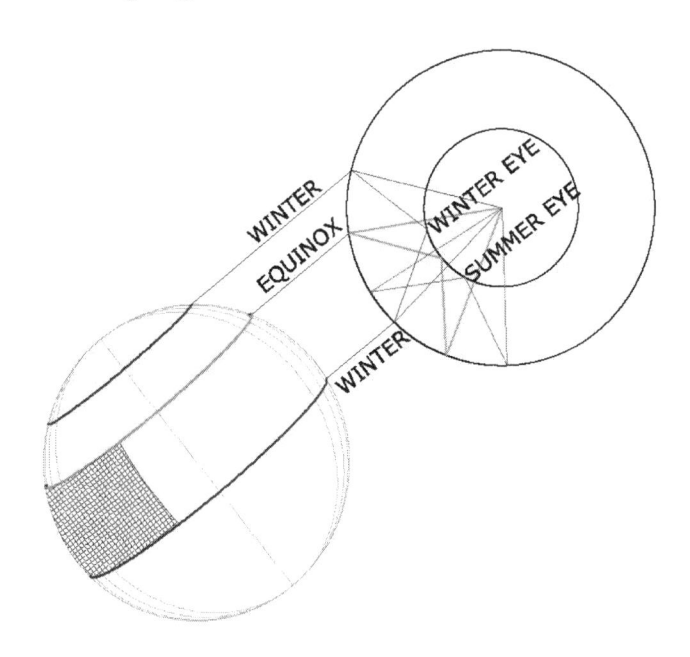

Ideal mirror zones for winter (6 month) period

In his book; 'Sustainable energy without the hot air', David MacKay, the current chief scientific adviser to the UK Department of Energy and Climate Change, looked at the possibility of paving some 5% of the UK countryside with solar panels.[06] One disadvantage of doing this is that the land cannot then be used for agriculture.

One alternative is to gather heat using widely spaced rows of *vertically* arranged spherical concentrators: This allows the land in-between to be used for agriculture during the three non-winter seasons.

It is possible that this sort of system may be necessary at some time in the future. If so, it is also possible that our ancestors may have provided future generations with a method of solving their energy needs.

APPENDIX B: Spherical solar collectors 119

Before Stonehenge

During 2008 and 2009, a number of frames were built to test out the principles of spherical solar collection.

At halfway between the polar centre (the hinge) and the mirrors, light was found to concentrate as predicted. The light will remain concentrated if the receptor is rotated continuously along an arc. After testing this using a very simple arrangement (a piece of timber with a car radiator stuck on the end), I built a second test arrangement out of plywood using larger mirror sets:

One of the early second stage proof tests (2008)

The car radiator was now enclosed with polystyrene and had two flexible pipes attached. A small pump circulated water to a household storage tank, and temperature sensors allowed me to measure how much heat was being gathered per hour.

For more detailed testing over autumn 2008 and winter 2009, the third and fourth series used a fabricated roller assembly set on a Virendeel steel arc. These were placed on the same timber frame, set to our latitude (51°), and moved up and down according to the season.

Stage 3 and 4 tests

The roller sets were moved mechanically around the arcs by a small motor device in the same way that a clock hand is moved around its face.

The roller assembly

Constructing and focusing the mirrors

APPENDIX B: Spherical solar collectors 121

The measured rate of collection in winter equates to about one kilowatt hour per day per square metre of mirror surface. This varies depending on the collection temperature. For instance, if collected at 80°C, the losses will be slightly higher than if collected at 50°C.

The principle of a rotating pole, moving within inwardly facing mirrors, resulted in all sorts of scheme designs to see how, and if, this could be used: Equatorial solar power plants (1), near-equator heat units (2), low cost portable cooking units (3), rigs for heating buildings in temperate zones (4), low cost drying and communal units (5) and simple portable steam sterilisation units (6):

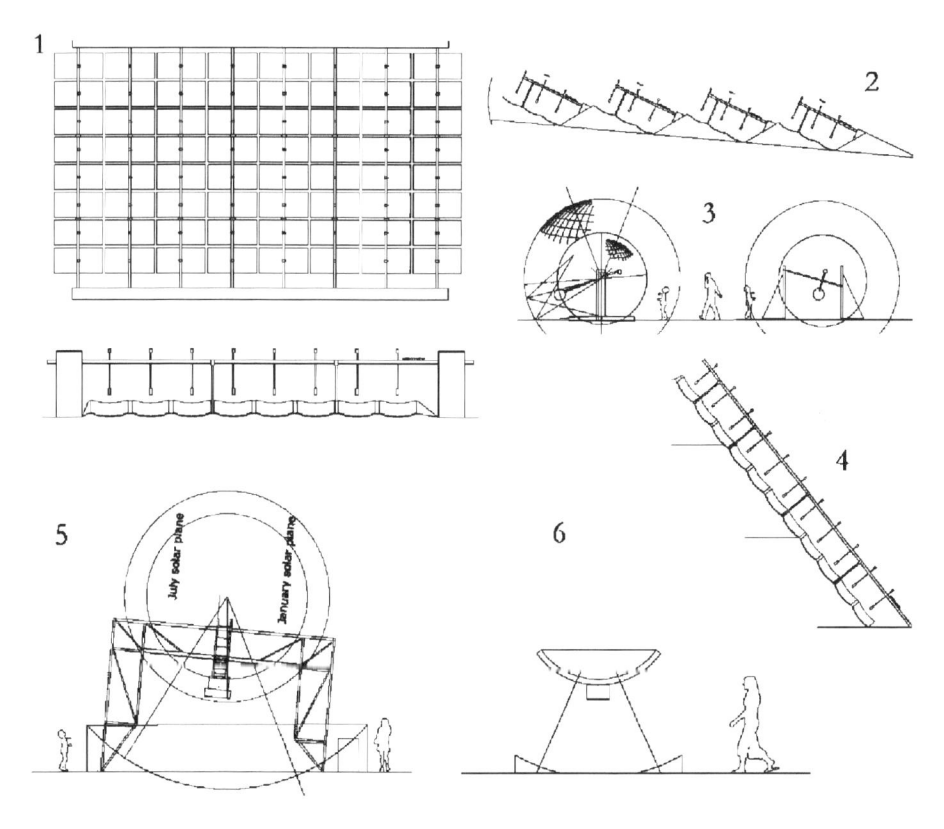

Preliminary scheme drawing extracts

Then, in 2010, whilst on a trip to visit my uncle in Salisbury, my boys wanted to visit Stonehenge. When we got there, I noticed that all the features of Stonehenge seemed to be the same as one of the forms of the later designs. So I built a computer 3D model of Stonehenge and then fitted the design in to see if there was any correlation. It was a precise fit:

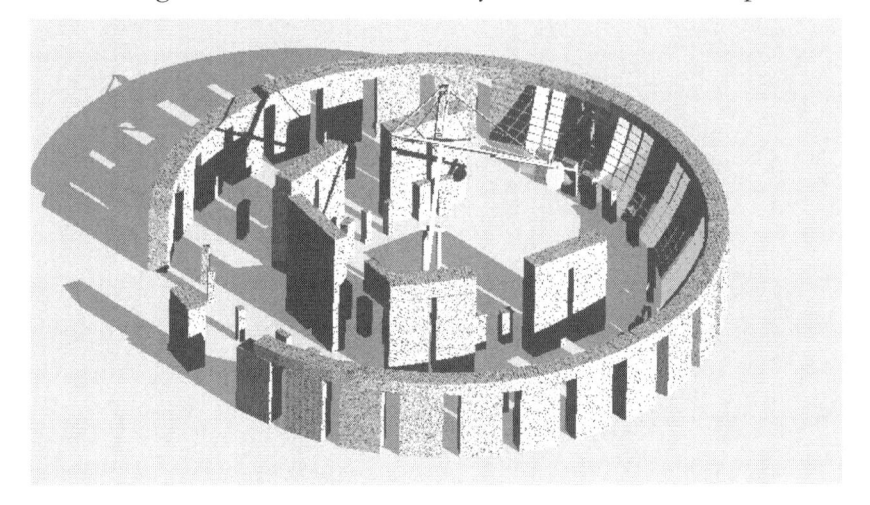

But the computer model predicted that there would have to be holes in the edge of a stone known as stone 54. So, with some trepidation, I booked a 'private viewing' of the inside of the circle.

Three holes existed, exactly in the locations predicted by the computer model:

Stone 54 at Stonehenge

APPENDIX B: Spherical solar collectors 123

I then modified the arrangement back to a pole and rod, the very first thing I had started with, and fitted a reflector:

Stage 5 tests: 2013

It was not at all surprising that this produced a 'miniature sun', so I duplicated the arrangement of Stonehenge in full to see if there was anything that could be learned:

This new arrangement was a series of timber frames, set out at about 30% scale, and arranged so that the pole would be in the equinox position:

Test frame 6: 2013

Each frame was tied using rope and pegged to the ground. The mirrors were then set out to the 'blue-stone' positions:

Test frame 6: 2013

APPENDIX B: Spherical solar collectors   125

The full arrangement clad in cloth:

Stage 6 tests: Willingdon, June 2013

Stay ropes were found to be necessary from 51/52, 57/58 and 59/60 to cover the full range of movement:

Stage 6 tests: Stay ropes seen from below, June 2013

Stay-rope trajectory for lowest set of the pole

The flat surfaces of the inner trilithons were found to be very useful when trying to get the mirrors focused. Lozenge type patterns form at these surfaces if the focus of the mirror set is not precisely correct:

Back-reflections: Stage 6 tests: Willingdon, June 2013

After testing, the equipment was packed away for solstice 2013.

NOTES & REFERENCES

Chapter 1 Notes

General introduction:
01: Henges peculiarity to Britain: Parker Pearson et al, 2012: 322
02: Henges exclusive to Britain: Dyer 1990: 64
03: Uniqueness of carving at Stonehenge: Pitts, 2001: 85
04: Weight of Stones: Johnson 2008: 136-7
05: Mortice and tenon work was first noted in Camden's Britannia of 1586: Johnson 2008: 46
06: Diameter of sarsen circle: Chippendale, 2004: 19
07: Weight of Stones: Johnson 2008: 136-7

The people:
11: Genetics of people; past to present: Darvill, 2006: 70
12: Boscombe Down: Johnson 2008: 30
13: Amesbury Archer: Johnson 2008: 29
14: Amesbury Archer: Parker-Pearson 2012: 213
15: Evidence for trade with continent Bronze age: Pryor, 2004: 296-297
16: Genetics: Parker-Pearson 2012: 19
17: Clothing: Parker-Pearson 2012: 15
18: Landscape: Souden, 1997: 103
19: Granaries and storage: Parker-Pearson 2012: 25
20: Elitist theories: Castleden 1987: 206-207
21: Rope use, houses and other materials: Parker-Pearson 2012: 16
22: 2300BC: Possible end date for long term use of Durrington using carbon dates: Parker-Pearson 2012: 117-118
23: Deer Antlers: Pitts, 2001: 186
24: Durrington feasting & construction phase: Parker-Pearson 2012: 110
25: Width and depth of river: Parker-Pearson 2012: 156
26: Boats 6-5000BC and Early Bronze Age: Pryor, 2004: 294
27: Wessex skulls: Castleden 1987: 194-195
28: Build & health of population: Castleden 1987: 195-198
29: Pig feasting & evidence of some summer occupation: Parker-Pearson 2012: 126
30: Stew & winter feasts: Burl, 2006: 164
31: Import of animals to Durrington:Parker-Pearson 2012: 120
32: Pig teeth & winter slaughter: Johnson 2008: 26

The path to Stonehenge:
41: Pre-Roman trails: Trevelyan, 1947: 8
42: Composite map compiled from: Wright, 1988: pages 10-30
43: Composite map compiled from: Trevelyan, 1947: 7-9
44: Composite map compiled from: Castleden, 1987: 115
45: South Downs National Park Authority. Website available at: http://www.nationaltrail.co.uk/southdowns/text.asp?PageId=30
46: South Downs track: Staveley, 2003: 3
47: Clearance: Butler, 2005: 2
48: The Sweet Track: Castleden, 1987: 118-119
49: Castleden, 1987: 115
50: Holes in former car park: Cleal *et al.* 1995: 43 & seq
51: Scheduled Monuments surrounding Stonehenge: Darvill, 2006: Preface (page 13)

Stonehenge: The word:
61: Hill, 2008: 22
62: Burl, 2006:225
63: Derivation of the word 'Henge': Mohen, 2002: 162
64: Kendrick: Pitts, 2001: 26
65: Stonehenge and the word 'henge': Pitts, 2001: 26 & 28
66: Meaning of Heng according to Stuckeley (Gallows): Burl, 2006: 19

A history of discovery
01: Deed of 937 AD: Hill, 2008: 21
02: Pepys Quote: Hill, 2008: 39
03: Defoe quote: Hill, 2008: 39
04: No Roman references: Hill, 2008: 39
05: Second wonder: Johnson 2008: 37
06: Historia Anglorum: Hill, 2008: 21
07: A digital scan of the work by Indigo Jones can be found at; http://digital.library.wisc.edu/1711.dl/DLDecArts.StoneHeng
08: John Aubrey: Johnson 2008: 55
09: Aubrey holes: Johnson 2008: 56-57
10: On William Stukeley: Johnson 2008: 61-66
11: On John Wood: Johnson 2008: 66 on
12: Stone numbering sequence: Johnson 2008: 123
13: Darwin's visit; Darvill, 2006: 45
14: Image from: Barclay, 1895: Plan I
15: Central Post Structure: Johnson 2008: 88
16: Gowland's suggestions; Darvill, 2006: 45
17: Image from: Barclay, 1895.

18: Richards, 2007: 160
19: Hawkins: Parker-Pearson 2012: 46 (but see also Hawkins reference)
20: Solstice: Hoyle 1977: 14
21: Sarmizegetusa (Grădiste): Hoyle 1977: 15
22: Solsticial alignment; other Great Henges; Parker-Pearson 2012: 342
23: Alignments and Ruggles: Parker-Pearson 2012: 48-49
24: Alignment: Johnson 2008: 176

A potted history of the monument's phases
31: Settlement size: Parker-Pearson 2012: 4 and 92
32: Durrington/Stonehenge simultaneity: Parker-Pearson 2012: 5
33: Mesolithic post location: Burl, 2006: 223
34: The car park holes & woodland: Johnson 2008: 114
35: Post hole dating: Darvill, 2006: 62 & location plan on page 64
36: Mesolithic post-hole dating: Parker-Pearson 2012: 135
37: 'Tamed Wildwood': Darvill, 2006: 24
38: Vegetation landscape: Darvill, 2006: 69
39: Great and Lesser Cursus: Burl, 2006: 84
40: Cursus Period: Parker Pearson et al, 2012: 323
41: Uniqueness of Cursuses to Britain: Parker-Pearson 2012: 144
42: Dating the Scottish cursuses: Parker-Pearson 2012: 144
43: Newgrange: O'Kelly 1998: 21
44: Knowth: Eogan 1986: 178
45: Alignments: Hutton1996: 4
46: Chronology revision: Parker-Pearson 2007: 627
47: C14 decay: Hoyle 1977: 25-26
48: Climatic conditions in third millennium BC: Darvill, 2006: 93
49: Grasslands & woods: Parker-Pearson 2012: 164
50: Internal post-holes: Johnson 2008: 110-113
51: Periglacial stripes: Parker-Pearson 2012: 245

Potted history: Stage 1
61: The Bank: Johnson 2008: 100
62: The counter-scarp bank: Johnson 2008: 101
63 Calibration of ditch: Parker-Pearson 2012: 43
64: Holes beneath the Bank Johnson 2008: 100-101
65: Entrances though the bank: Johnson 2008: 102
66: The southern entrance though the bank: Johnson 2008: 104
67: Stage 1: New Phasing: Parker Pearson et al, 2012: 309
68: Time-line: Parker-Pearson 2012: 7
69: Level of Aubrey Holes: Johnson 2008: 108
70: Aubrey Holes: Johnson 2008: 104-109

71: Entry through bank relocated: Dyer 1990: 66
72: Chalk Plaques: Parker-Pearson 2012: 227

Potted history: Stage 2 to 5
81: Q&R incompleteness: Parker-Pearson 2012: 169 and dating: 310
82: Q&R hole rings: Johnson 2008: 129-134
83: Lintels on Q&R settings: Johnson 2008: 132
84: Ring within R ring: Johnson 2008: 131 (see figure text)
85: Ditch around the Heel-stone: Pitts, 2001: 139
86: Stone hole 97: Johnson 2008: 118 Note also similarity to North and south barrows: 120
87: Solar rise over Heel-stone: Burl, 2006: 113
88: Stage 3: New Phasing: Parker Pearson et al, 2012: 310
89: Presence of sarsen below Avenue banks: Parker-Pearson 2012: 247-248
90: Image from: Barclay, 1895.
91: Quotation regarding Avenue: Parker Pearson et al, 2012: 242
92: Avenue bend (absence of hollows): Field 2012: 34-35
93: Stage 4: New Phasing: Parker Pearson et al, 2012: 311
94: Y&Z: Johnson 2008: 167
95: Y&Z holes: Dating and contents: Darvill, 2006: 164

The Stones: A potted summary
01: Tonnage of Stone: Richards, 2007: 207
02: Silica in sandstone: Richards, 2004: 5
03: Sarsen structure: Darvill, 2006: 131
04: Evelyn Quote: Burl, 2006: 9
05: Glaciers: Parker-Pearson 2012: 63
06: Hill, 2008: 13
07: Geoffrey of Monmouth's history was in Latin and dated 1136 and also known by the name *Historia Regum Britanniae*.
08: Sarcens buried: Parker-Pearson 2012: 294
09: Transport distance: Burl, 2006: 168
10: Sarsen shaping: Darvill, 2006: 131
11: Use of Mauls: Richards, 2007: 207
12: Weight of mauls: Pitts, 2001: 85
13: Stone preparation (evidence for): Parker-Pearson 2012: 42
14: Level top: Uprights different lengths: Burl, 2006: 168
15: Chippendale, 2004: 19
16: Height of trilithon stones: Johnson 2008: 143
17: Faces look inwards: Johnson 2008: 144
18: Sarsens worked more finely on inside faces: Hill, 2008: 44
19: Architectural device of entasis: Burl, 2006: 35

20: Level top of lintels: Chippendale, 2004: 19
21: Trilithon surfaces: Johnson 2008: 137
22: Uniqueness of Great Trilithon outer facing surface: Johnson 2008: 139
23: Height of trilithons: Johnson 2008: 136, *but note burl (p 176) has noted different dimensions (6.1, 6.5 and 7.3m respectively)*
24: Mortise and tenon joints: Darvill, 2006: 125
25: Position of stone 56: Johnson 2008: 240 & 244
26: Position of Stone 56: Parker-Pearson 2012: 256
27: Dating the Trilithons: Parker-Pearson 2012: 132
28: Foot of Stone: Pitts, 2001: 157
29: Stone 54 packing: Johnson 2008: 129
30: Outer bluestone circle diameter: Johnson 2008: 158
31: Bluestone variability below ground Cleal et al. 1995: 28 check this refers to outer ring
32: Outer bluestone height & spacing: Johnson 2008: 158
33: Bluestone outer ring not dressed Cleal et al. 1995: 27
34: Stone 36: lintel: Johnson 2008: 159
35: Inner bluestone height and spacing: Johnson 2008: 162
36: Inner horse-shoe grading: Burl, 2006: 179
37: Inner bluestone oval: Johnson 2008: 161
38: Best stones in inner circle: Burl, 2006: 177
39: Inner bluestone previous arrangements: Johnson 2008: 163

The axis of the monument
01: Post-holes at entry: Cleal et al. 1995: 142-143. see also 269
02: Bearing of Avenue: Burl, 2006: 189
03: Causeway post holes and post holes at A: Johnson 2008: 173
04: Stone hole numbering at entry: Cleal et al. 1995: 269
05: Chippendale, 2004: 124
06: Slaughter Stone: Johnson 2008: 151
07: Slaughter stone shaping: Burl, 2006: 187
08: D&E holes: Johnson 2008: 152
09: 97 & Heel-stone: Cleal et al. 1995: 289
10: Sequence: Ditch around 96 intersecting 97: Pitts, 1992: 149
11: Stone 97 pit: Parker-Pearson 2012: 42
12: Parallelogram of Station Stones: Burl, 2006: 151
13: North and South Barrows: Johnson 2008: 148-150
14: Wyeth, 2001: 5
15: Observations by Ruggles: Alignment to the moon: Burl, 2006: 154

Metals and Stonehenge
01: Traces of copper at footing of Stone 56: Chippendale, 2004: 168
02: Metal & copper at Durrington: Parker-Pearson 2012: 125
03: Metal trading networks Johnson 2008: 121
04: Tin tablet: Burl, 2006: 22
05: Copper and tin: Johnson 2008: 24
06: Dating the Copper Age: Parker-Pearson 2012: 123-126
07: Sources of metals: Gerrard, 2000: 14
08: Copper in Turkey: Roberts 1980: 52
09: Mirrors; earliest use of: Prendergast 2003, 3
10: Penhallurick 1986: 183-4

New Evidence
01: Abbott *et al*, 2012: 59.
02: Abbott *et al*, 2012: 21
03: Abbott *et al*, 2012: 21
04: Abbott *et al*, 2012: 51
05: Abbott *et al*, 2012: 21
06: Abbott *et al*, 2012: 23
07: Abbott *et al*, 2012: 52
08: Abbott *et al*, 2012: 23

Theories
01: Theory quote Johnson 2008: 91
02: Burl, 1979: 200
03: Early theories: Johnson 2008: 58-59
04: Theories: Hancock, 1998: xiv
05: Temple to the goddess: Meaden, 1992: 166
06: Hawkins 1974: Preface
07: Errors of alignment in Hawkins: Hoyle 1977: 55
08: Astronomical alignments: Hoyle 1977: 65
09: No account in documented history: Hoyle 1977: 91
10: Moon and early Stonehenge: Darvill, 2006: 143
11: Alignment theories: Pitts, 2001: 227

Chapter 2 Notes

01: Scheduled monument details can be found at:
http://www.pastscape.org.uk/
02: Schmidt-Kaler and W. Schlosser 1984: 183
03: Johnson 2008: 96
04: Arecibo Observatory in Arecibo, Puerto Rico.
05: Abbott *et al*, 2012: 59. Weight of Stone 54 = 29 tons (assumed to be UK tons but this is not stated in the report). By comparison a 14 metre, 300mm pine pole weighs approximately 0.55 UK tons.

Chapter 3 Notes

01: Prosser & Raw 2000
02: Scheduled and other monument details can be found at:
http://www.pastscape.org.uk/
03: Curwen 1929: 209
04: The word Bourne can also mean spring.
05: From discussions with local historians, the name Polegate seems to have existed prior to modern development.

Chapter 4 Notes

01: Troyes, (c. 1160-1180)
02: Baillie 2005: 208

Chapter 5 Notes

01: Anaximander: Lawson 2004: 91
02: Ptolemy: Lawson 2004: 34
03: Public Domain work by Bartolomeu Velho in 1568. A copy is accessible at:
http://en.wikipedia.org/wiki/File:Bartolomeu_Velho_1568.jpg
04: Aristarchus: Lawson 2004: 19-20
05: Aristarchus: Lawson 2004: 32-33
06: Aristarchus: Lawson 2004: 33
07: Public Domain work by Andreas Cellarius. Illustration of the Copernican system, from the Harmonia Macrocosmica (1660). A copy is accessible at:
http://en.wikipedia.org/wiki/File:Heliocentric.jpg
08: Public Domain work by William Cuningham. known as the "Coelifer Atlas" from The Cosmographical Glasse of 1559. A similar copy is accessible at:
http://www.loc.gov/exhibits/world/heavens.html
09: Johnson 2008: 101

11: If the winter founding point is initially set as being approximately one half radius (ie 8m for a 32m diameter bowl), so that platforms can be used for access to the end of the rod, then the height of the centre of the mirror-bowl above ground will be 8m x tan (51°) = 9.88m

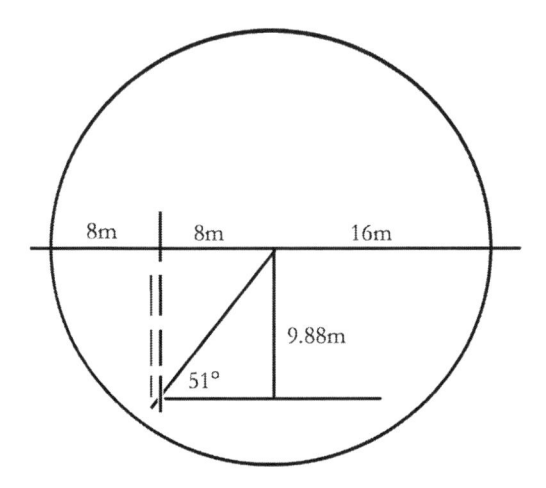

12: In winter at a 51° latitude, the maximum angle of the sun would have been about 15° in 2400BC (see appendix A). The rod will be pointing upwards by 24° relative to a perpendicular to the polar axis: The effect of this is that the rod must point *down* by 15° relative to the horizon (39°-24°): Because the apparatus is invertedly mimicking the sun, the fact that it is pointing down by 15°, when the sun is up above the horizon by 15°, is no surprise.

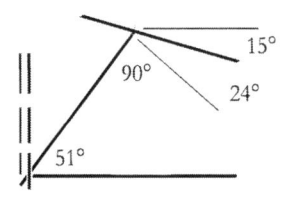

13: If the apparatus is pointing down by 15° over 9 metres, the centre of the mirror-bowl must be at least 9m x sin(15°) above the top of the rim: 2.33 metres. At a viewing angle of say up to 10° (see note below for explanation), an additional allowance of approx 9m x tan (10°) must be made because the end of the rod is set back from the rim: This adds 1.59 metres. Allowing for the size of the reflector adds a third of a metre. Another effect (in summer: see notes below) lowers the required maximum height by about 0.53 metres.

NOTES & REFERENCES 135

In total, the height of the rim must be at least 4.8 metres or so below the mirror-bowl centre (2.33 + 1.59 + 0.33 + 0.53 = 4.78m).

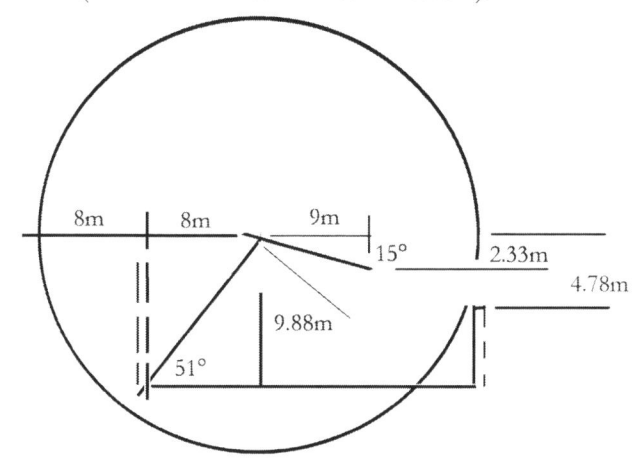

14: The viewing angle has been taken as up to 10°: This is an arbitrary selection because if people were made to stand, or say if children were excluded, the viewing angle could be a lot less than 10°. In this particular case, an angle of 10° seems appropriate because this equates to the start of the Avenue, just outside the bank of Stonehenge: Anyone allowed into the area within the bank could be able to see the effect from within the stones themselves; and anyone sitting around the bank would be able to see the same thing, even at its lowest point:

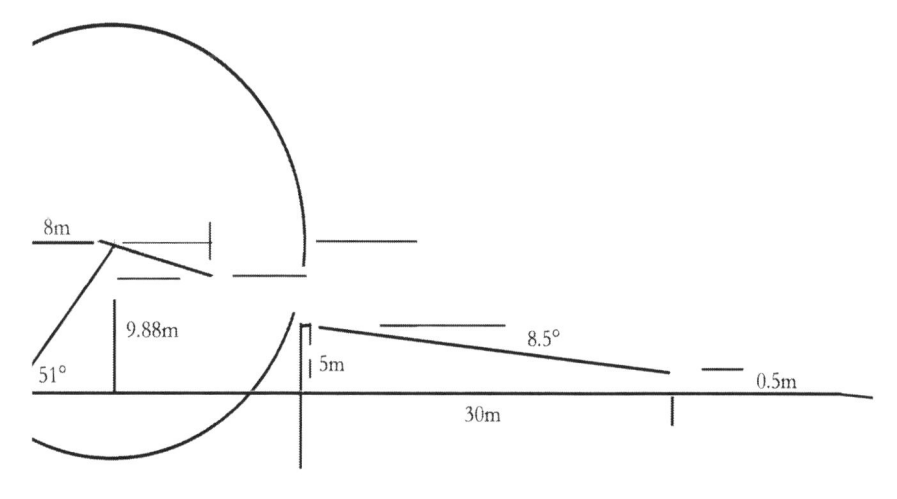

15: In summer at a 51° latitude, the maximum angle of the sun would have been about 15° in 2400BC (see appendix A). The rod will be pointing downwards by 24° relative to a perpendicular to the polar axis: The effect of this is that it will point down by 39°+24° = 63°: Because the apparatus is mimicking the sun, the rod must point down by 63° from the horizon's plane when the sun is up above the horizon by 63°:

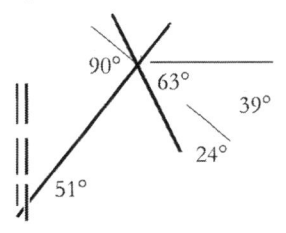

16: If the apparatus is pointing down by 63° in summer, this will extend the distance to the reflector when seen at an angle. The extended distance is 16m - 9m x cos (63°) = [16m - 4m] = 12m approx. For a viewing angle of 10°, This makes approx 12m x tan (10°) = 2.11 metres (note that in the picture below, we are only concerned with the distance: The assembly also moves up in the summer months (see notes below)

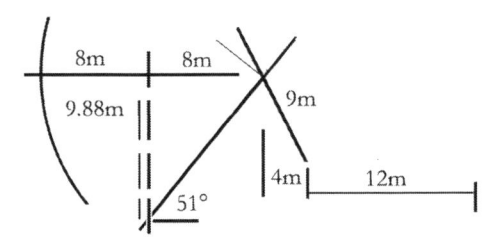

17: Given the parameters in the preceding notes, the height of the mirror-bowl rim *must not exceed* 9.88m -4.79m = 5.09m

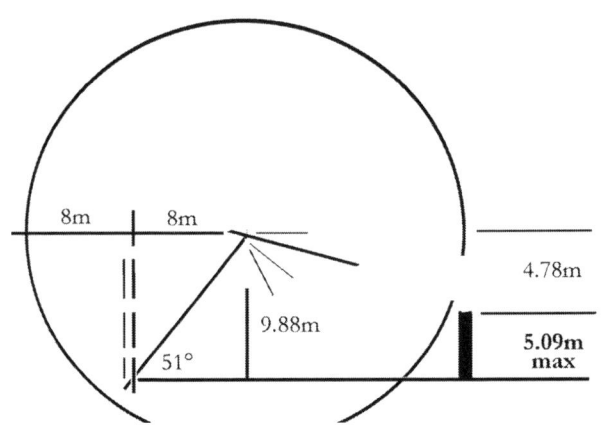

NOTES & REFERENCES   137

18: The inner rim diameter, for a 32m bowl diameter, must not exceed 30m because of the intersection with the rim (at a height of 5m or so):

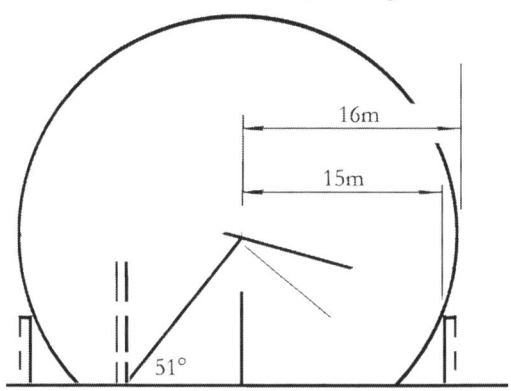

19: This note is calculated from the vertical range of the end of the sail when moved over the distance and multiplied by the difference between the polar position factors. In this case (8m + 1m) x (2 x sin (24°)) x cos (51°) x 90 % = 4.15m

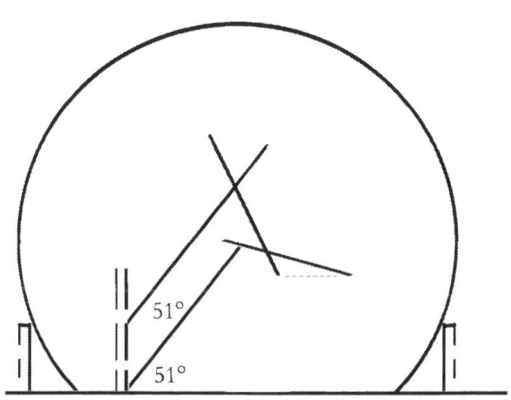

20: Using a pine post, 3-400mm diameter with a 14m length and allowing up to 1000kg weight, the lateral 'kick' force at the uppermost socket could be up to 10kN (for example if ropes are used for the final lift from say 30°to 51°). This results in an overturning moment at the base of up to 50kNm when lifting using the uppermost socket. The resistance of this (heaviest) stone is 284kN (see chap 2, note 5) multiplied by its lever arm in the short axis; >100kNm resistance.

138 STONEHENGE

21: The bowls for each position at Stonehenge are illustrated in this diagram:

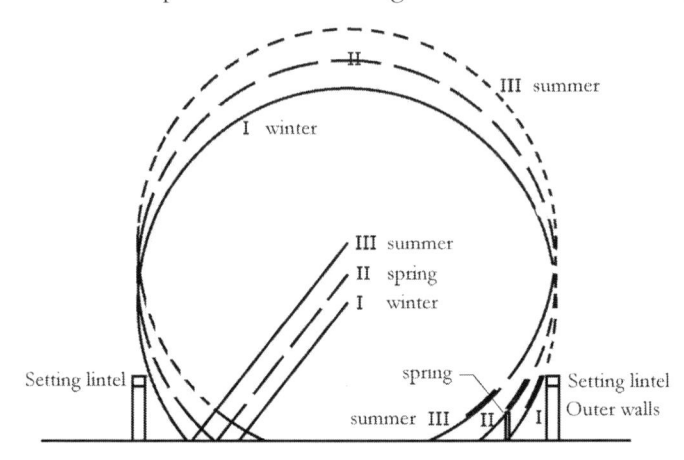

22: Illustration (showing the Great Trilithon & support for pole removed) to show possible drop-down for a timer-ring:

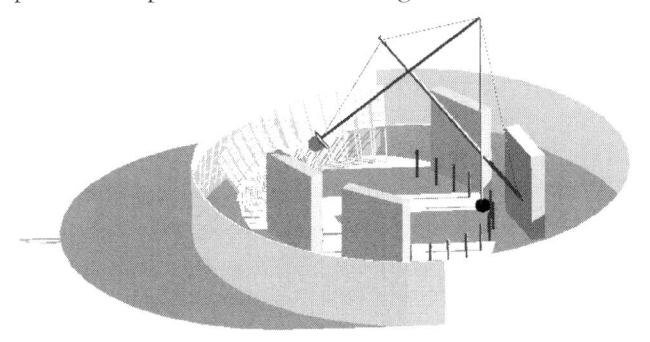

23: The Chief's Face was discovered by Terence Meaden in 1999 and reported by BBC news at:
http://news.bbc.co.uk/1/hi/sci/tech/474977.stm

24: A geocentric world is shown in more detail, locating where Salisbury and Stonehenge are positioned, in the illustration below:

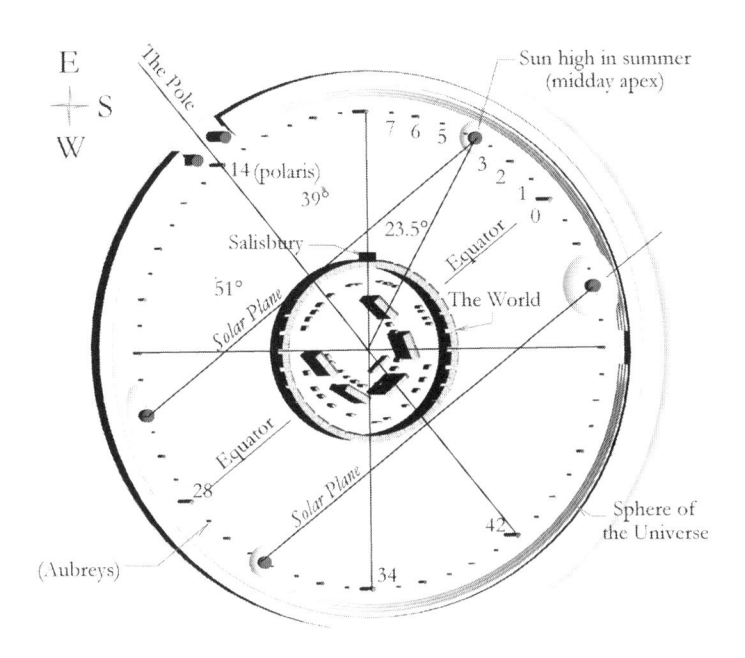

25: Hutton 1996: 6: *"Yule in Old Norse is Yol, Swedish jul and Danish juul. The derivation baffles linguists and is possibly related to the Gothic 'Huel' or Anglo-Saxon 'Hweal', meaning 'Wheel'. Another explanation is that it means 'Jolly'."*
26: Diodorus Siculus, Library of History 5.67.06
27: Diodorus Siculus, Library of History 2.47.05

Notes for Epilogue and Appendices:

01: See: http://www.istp.gsfc.nasa.gov/stargaze/Sprecess.htm
02: Berger 1976 133. A copy may be accessed here:
    http://adsabs.harvard.edu/abs/1976A&A....51..127B
03: See: http://en.wikipedia.org/wiki/Solar_irradiation#Solar_constant
04: See: http://en.wikipedia.org/wiki/Airmass#Airmass_and_solar_energy
05: See: http://en.wikipedia.org/wiki/Ozone_layer
06: Page 41: 'Sustainable Energy – without the hot air' can currently (2013) be downloaded as a free .pdf at: http://www.withouthotair.com/

References

Abbott, M., Anderson-Whymark, H. *et al. Stonehenge Laser Scan: Archaeological Analysis Report 6457*. English Heritage, London, 2012

Barclay, E. *Stonehenge and Its Earth-works*. D. Nutt, London, 1895

Berger, A. L *Obliquity and precession for the last 5 000 000 years*. Astronomy and Astrophysics, vol. 51, no. 1, Aug. 1976. p. 127-135.

Burl, A. *Prehistoric Avebury*, Yale University Press, Ltd., London, 1979

Burl, A. *Stonehenge: A new History of the World's Greatest Stone Circle*. Constable & Robinson Ltd, London, 2006

Baillie, M. and P McCafferty, P. *The Celtic Gods*, Tempus Publishing Limited, Stroud, 2005

Balfour, M. *Stonehenge and its Mysteries*. Hutchinson and Co., London, 1983

Butler, C. *An interim report on recent excavations at the Long Man, Wilmington, East Sussex*, 2005

Castleden, R. *The Stonehenge People*, Routledge & Kegan Paul Ltd, London, 1987

Chippendale, C. *Stonehenge Complete*. Thames and Hudson Inc. New York, 2004

Cleal, R. M. J. Walker, K. E. and Montague, R. *Stonehenge in Its Landscape*. English Heritage, London, 1995

Curwen, E.C. *Neolithic Camp, Combe Hill, Jevington*, SAC Vol. 70 1929

Darvill, T: *Stonehenge: The Biography of a Landscape*. Tempus Publishing Limited, Stroud, 2006

Dyer, J. *Ancient Britain*. B. T. Batsford Limited, London, 1990

Eogan, G. *Knowth and the passage-tombs of Ireland*, Thames and Hudson Ltd, London, 1986

Field et al, *The Avenue and Stonehenge: Archaeological Survey Report: Series no. 31-2012*, English Heritage, Portsmouth, 2012

Gerrard, S. *The Early British Tin Industry*, Tempus Publishing Limited, Stroud, 2000

Hancock, G. and Faiia, S. *Heaven's Mirror: Quest for the Lost Civilisation*, The Penguin Group, London, 1998

Hawkins, G. S. *Stonehenge Decoded*. Souvenir Press Ltd, Great Britain, 1974

Hill, R.H *Stonehenge*. Profile Books, London, 2008.

Hoyle, F. *On Stonehenge*. Heinemann Educational Books, London, 1977

Hutton, R. *The Stations of The Sun*. Oxford University Press, Oxford, 1996

Johnson, A. *Solving Stonehenge: The New Key to an Ancient Enigma*. Thames & Hudson, London, 2008

Lawson, R. M. *Science in the Ancient World: An Encyclopedia*. ABC-CLIO, California, 2004

Loomis, R.S. *Celtic Myth and Arthurian Romance*. Academy Chicago Publishers, 1997

Meaden, G. T. *The Stonehenge Solution*. Souvenir Press Ltd., London, 1992

Mohen, J-P. *Standing Stones: Stonehenge, Carnac and the World of Megaliths*. Thames and Hudson, London, 2002.

Monmouth, G. *Historia Regum Britanniae (English: The History of the Kings of Britain)* c. 1136

O'Kelly, M. K.*Newgrange*. Thames and Hudson, London 1982, 1998

Parker-Pearson, M. and The Stonehenge Riverside Project. *Stonehenge: Exploring the Greatest Stone Age Mystery*. Simon and Schuster, London, 2012

Parker-Pearson, M. et al. *The Age of Stonehenge*. Antiquity 81 (2007): 617-639

Penhallurick, R D. *Tin in Antiquity: Its Mining and Trade Throughout the Ancient World with Particular Reference to Cornwall*. Maney Publishing, 1986

Pitts, M. *Hengeworld*. Arrow Books, London, 2001

Prendergast, M. *Mirror, Mirror*. Basic Books, New York, 2003

Prosser, R. & Raw, M. *Landmark AS Geography*. Collins Educational, London, 2000

Pryor, F. *Britain BC*. Harper Perennial, London, 2004

Richards, J. *Stonehenge: The Story So Far.* English Heritage, Swindon, 2007.

Richards, J. *Stonehenge: A History in Photographs.* English Heritage, London, 2004.

Roberts, J. M. *The Pelican History of The World.* Penguin Books, Middlesex, UK, 1980

Schmidt-Kaler, T.H. and Schlosser, W. *Stone Age Burials as a hint to Prehistoric Astronomy.* Royal Astronomical Society of Canada, 78, 178. (1984) "Astronomie vor 5000"

Souden, D. *Stonehenge: Mysteries of the Stones and Landscape.* Collins and Brown, London, 1997.

Staveley, D. *A Resistivity Survey of Combe Hill Causewayed Enclosure Near Willingdon, East Sussex.* 2003

Trevelyan, G.M. *History of England.* Longmans, Green and Co. Ltd., London, 1947

Troyes, C. *Perceval le Gallois, ou le Conte du Graal,* c. 1160-1180)

Wright, G.N. *Roads and Trackways of Wessex.* Moorland Publishing Co Ltd, Derbyshire, 1988

Wyeth, R. *The Stonehenge Story.* Gemini, Wiltshire, 2001

INDEX

24°; 38, 39, 44, 49, 57, 80, 94, 108, 110
3D model; 122
51°; 38, 44, 52, 83, 93, 94, 96, 98, 111, 119
Aceribo Observatory; 55
Advanced Research Projects Agency; 114
Africa; 21
Air Force Cambridge Research Laboratory; 114
Air Mass; 109
Alderamin; 107
alignment; 11-18, 25, 26, 32, 33, 50, 51, 105
alloy; 34
Alrai; 107
Amesbury Archer; 2
amphitheatre; 82-84
Anaraith; 32
Anaximander of Miletus; 91
Ancient Greeks; 104
antler; 3, 15
Apollo; 104, 106
architecture; 22
Arecibo Observatory; 114
Aristarchus of Samos; 92
Aristotle; 92
Arthurian; 86, 87, 104
astronomy; 11, 26, 32, 36, 105
Atkinson, Richard ; 10
Aubrey holes; 8, 11, 16, 26, 48, 93, 94
Aubrey, John; 8
Avebury; 4, 21, 32, 94
Avenue; 11, 16, 18, 19, 25, 31, 48, 50, 51, 57, 83, 93, 101

axial tilt; 23, 60, 80, 84, 98, 108
Babylon Down; 78
bank; 6, 8, 15, 16, 19, 22, 25, 33, 48, 93, 94
Barclay, Edgar; 9, 10, 19
barrow; 19, 26, 27, 83
Beachy Brow; 73-75
Beachy Head; 41, 46, 69-71, 73, 75, 81, 84
Beaker; 27
bearing; 25, 86
Bell Tout lighthouse; 69
Big Dipper; 107
bluestone; 17, 19-22, 24, 26, 60, 61, 99, 100
Boscombe Down; 2
Bourne Hill; 41, 42, 71, 73-78, 81, 84
Bronze Age; 2, 3, 5, 27, 34
Burl, Aubrey; 18
Butser Hill; 5
Cæsar; 89
Camden, William; 27
Camelot; 87
Cancer; 93
Capricorn; 93
carbon; 3, 12, 13, 15, 28
cardinal; 16, 46, 48, 50
cassiterite; 27, 28, 35
Çatal Hüyük; 27
Cauldron of the Dagda; 89
chalk plaques; 16
Chief's Face, the; 100
Chilterns; 4
Christchurch; 5
CIBSE Design Guide A; 112
circle; 1, 10, 16-18, 20-24, 26, 31, 38,

43-47, 49-51, 56, 60, 77, 80, 82, 93, 96, 98, 99, 107, 108, 110, 111, 113, 116, 117, 122
clothing; 2
Coast; 5, 40, 42, 101
Cold Crouch; 78
Combe Hill; 5, 78-81, 84
concentrator; 65, 87, 88, 97, 101, 102, 118
Copernicus; 92
copper; 2, 27, 28, 34, 35, 54, 57
Cornwall; 27, 28, 35
Cotswolds; 4
counter-scarp bank; 15
Cuningham, William ; 93
Curiosity; 27, 35
cursus; 8, 12-14, 16, 105
D and E holes; 8, 18, 19, 25, 27, 87
Darwin, Charles ; 9
De Bello Gallico; 89
De revolutionibus orbium coelestium; 92
De Situ Orbis; 89
De Troyes, Chrétien; 86, 88, 90
Defoe, Daniel; 8
Deneb; 107
Department of Energy and Climate Change; 118
dolerite; 17
druid; 8, 9, 27, 32, 89, 90
Durrington; 3, 5, 12, 27
earthwork; 5
east; 1, 3, 9, 15-19, 29, 31, 37, 41-44, 46-48, 50, 57, 62, 64, 67, 68, 70, 71, 78, 81-84, 93, 97, 99, 101
Eastbourne; 5, 70, 84
eclipses; 11, 32
Ecliptic; 108, 110
Elliptic; 100, 108
enclosure; 1

English Heritage; 29
engraving; 29
entasis; 22
entrance; 15
equator; 37-39, 44, 46, 49, 52, 53, 93, 94, 109-111, 121
equinox; 13, 14, 38, 41, 46, 57, 60, 63, 68, 76, 77, 98, 99, 105, 109-112, 117, 124
Etymology; 6, 7, 18, 84, 102
Europe; 1-3, 5, 6, 12, 27, 111
Evelyn, John ; 21
experiment to find curvature of the Earth; 39
experiment to find curvature with longitude; 42
experiment to find shape of earth with latitude; 39
experiment to find the north star; 36
experiment to find the rotation of the heavens; 37
experiment to track solar movement; 38
experiment to track stars; 37
farming; 12, 35
feasting; 3
Fir Bog'; 88
Fisher King; 86
flake; 22
Folkington Hill; 81
Four Treasures of the Tuatha Dé Danann; 89, 90
Foxholes Brow; 73, 74
genetics; 2
geocentric; 34, 43, 44, 48, 52-54, 56, 66, 67, 85, 88-93, 95, 97, 101, 104, 105
Geoffrey of Monmouth; 21
Gerrard, Sandy; 27
glacier; 2, 21

INDEX

Gordon, William E.; 114
Gowland, William; 10, 27
graal; 86
grail; 85-88, 90
granite; 21
grassland; 12
Great Ridgeway; 4
Greek; 9, 18, 35, 89, 104, 107
Greenwich Observatory; 52
Guardians of the (North) Pole, the; 107
Halley, Edmund ; 8
Hancock, Graham; 32
Harrow Way; 4
hauling; 97
Hawkins, Gerald ; 11, 32
Hawley, William; 10
haze; 40
hazel; 12, 35
heel; 18, 26, 91, 93, 102, 111, 112
Heel-stone; 18, 25, 26, 50, 93
heliocentric; 92
Helios; 18
Henge; 1, 6, 7, 15, 25, 102
Henry of Huntingdon; 8
Herstmonceux; 53
hinge; 6, 7, 34, 36, 43, 90, 96, 97, 99, 102, 119
Historia Anglorum; 8
history; 8, 12, 15, 17, 19, 20, 32, 90, 102
History of the Kings of Britain; 21
horizon; 8, 11, 14, 15, 26, 39, 40, 42, 46, 47, 50, 52, 68, 69, 71, 72, 76, 77, 83
horse-shoe; 1, 20, 24, 31, 61, 97, 99, 100
Hoyle, Fred; 11, 32
hunter-gatherer; 2
hwēol; 18

Hyperborea; 104
Hyperion; 104
ice Age; 2, 21
Icknield Way; 4
illusions; 47
In Beam irradiation; 109
Indian Circle; 46, 47
Ireland; 2, 13, 14, 21, 88, 90
Jevington; 81
Johnson, Anthony; 11, 32, 33
Jones, Indigo; 8
Kendrick, Thomas; 6
King Charles the Second; 8
King James the First; 8
Knowth; 13, 14, 16
Kochab; 107
Lake District, the; 2
landscape; 2, 12
language; 6, 7, 101
latitude; 26, 38, 44, 47, 49, 52, 83, 94, 95, 109, 111, 118, 119
Leonardo da Vinci; 103
level; 4, 16, 22, 23, 41, 56, 58, 60, 62, 69-72, 96, 109, 111
lintel; 1, 10, 17, 22-24, 31, 56, 59, 95, 96, 98, 99
Long Man, the; 82, 84
Low, Ward; 114
lozenge; 126
MacKay, David; 118
Marlborough Plain; 21
maul; 22, 35
May Pole; 58
Meaden, Terence; 30, 32, 100
megalith; 1, 18, 22
metal; 6, 27, 28, 34, 35, 54, 57, 65, 86, 88, 101, 103
migration; 2
mining; 4, 28, 35
mirror frame; 96

mortice and tenon; 23
Mynydd Preseli; 21
Newgrange; 13, 14, 16
Newgrange seen from Knowth: Ireland; 14
Newton, Issac ; 8
North Downs; 4
North pole; 35, 36, 38, 52, 101, 107, 108
North Star; 43, 44, 46, 50, 52, 56, 59, 86, 88, 107
North, John; 11
Northern Hemisphere; 38, 108, 109
number sequence of the stones; 9
oak; 12, 28
Observatory; 11, 32, 33, 52, 55, 114
obsidian; 27
Old Sarum; 4
old way; 106
optical illusion; 22
orbit; 35, 43, 44, 48, 49, 80, 107-110, 116
oval; 20, 24, 50
parabola; 113-115
Pashley Hill; 73, 75
passage tomb; 13
Pearson, Parker ; 19, 27-29
Penhallurick, Roger; 28
people; 2, 3, 6, 8, 12, 18, 29, 35, 57, 66, 72, 84, 90, 95, 103, 104, 106
Pepys, Samuel; 8
Perceval; 86
Petrie, Flinders ; 9
Pherkab; 107
Philolaus; 92
Phoenice; 107
Phonecians; 32
pick-axes; 3, 15
pig teeth; 3
Piggott, Stuart; 13

Pilgrim's Way; 4
pine; 7, 12, 72
Pitts, Mike; 18
Pliny; 90
plumb-bob; 46, 50, 51, 59
polar axis; 36, 39, 44, 48, 50, 52, 62, 81, 84, 93, 95, 96, 108, 111
Polaris; 107
Polegate; 84
Pomponius Mela; 89
processions; 19
Pryor, Francis; 3
Ptolemy; 91, 92
pyramid; 34
Pythagoras; 89
Pythagorus; 92
Q and R holes; 17, 20, 99
quartz; 21
Queen Boadicea; 32
radiation; 109, 115
radiator; 119
radio carbon; 3
renewable energy; 34
River Avon; 3
Roman; 5, 6, 8, 11, 32, 35, 87, 89
rope; 3, 69, 72, 124, 126
Ruggles, Clive; 11, 26, 32, 33
sailing; 3
Salisbury; 4, 21, 44, 47, 122
Sarmizegetusa; 11
sarsen; 1, 10, 17-24, 26, 31, 50, 95, 96
Saxon; 6
scanning; 10, 101
shadow; 46, 47, 51, 62, 97, 109, 111
siliceous cement; 21
sinusoidal; 98, 110, 111
Slaughter-stone; 19, 25, 50
smooth; 23, 99
socket; 52, 56, 58, 59, 96, 98-100
solar energy density; 109

INDEX

solar plane; 93, 98, 108, 110, 111, 117
solar sweep; 117
solstice; 1, 8, 11, 13-16, 18, 26, 33, 48, 93, 94, 102, 105, 106, 110, 111
South Downs; 5, 67, 69, 71-73, 75, 78, 81
Southern England; 36, 38, 42, 45, 53, 57
Spear of Lug; 89
sphere; 13, 36, 38, 39, 42-44, 55, 56, 66, 82, 92, 95-97, 108, 109, 113, 116
spherical; 55, 56, 60, 91, 97, 99, 104, 113-119
St Catherine's hill; 42
Station Stones; 18, 19, 26, 48, 93, 94
statistics; 13
Stone 11; 31
Stone 21; 31
Stone 36; 24
Stone 4; 29
stone 53; 29, 30, 56, 100
stone 54; 24, 30, 31, 52, 58, 59, 96, 98, 100, 122
Stone Age; 29, 34
stone hole 96; 25, 26
Stone hole 97; 18, 25, 26
Stone of Fál; 89
Stonehenge in its Landscape; 10
Stonehenge Laser Scan: Archaeological Investigation Report; 29
Stonehenge Riverside Project; 10, 29
Stuckeley, William; 8, 9, 19, 22, 27
Sunrise; 1, 11, 26, 40, 41, 46, 68, 69, 76, 77
Sussex; 53, 67, 79, 82
Sustainable energy without the hot air; 118
Sword of Light; 89

Swyre Head; 42
symmetry; 11, 17, 25, 26, 29, 31
T shape; 29, 30
tablet of tin; 27, 101
The Age of Stonehenge; 13
The Cosmographical Glasse; 93
The three season device; 57, 63, 113
theories; 32
Thuban; 36, 51
tin; 4, 6, 7, 27, 28, 34, 35, 54, 57, 65, 101-103
tin mining; 4
tin pest; 54
tons; 1, 2, 21-23, 25
track-way; 4, 5, 73
trade; 2, 27
transport; 21
tree-pole; 50, 86, 88, 96-99, 106
trilithon; 8, 10, 17, 19, 20, 23, 24, 27, 62, 63, 97, 99, 100, 126
Tuatha Dé Danann; 88-90
Universe; 34-38, 43-45, 48, 49, 52, 56, 66, 67, 82, 84, 85, 89-91, 94, 95, 102, 104-106, 116
upright; 22-25, 99
Uther Pendragon; 32
Vega; 107
Victorians; 97
visitor's car park; 5, 12
Wales; 2, 21
Well Combe; 75
Wessex; 3, 11
Wessex skulls; 3
Willian Stuckely; 6
Wilmington Hill; 81
Winchester; 4, 5
Windover Hill; 81, 82
Winn's oak; 28
Wood, John; 9
woodland; 12, 35

woodworking; 1
world: shape of; 40
Y and Z holes; 20

Yule; 102, 106
zodiac; 93

Illustrations

- Stonehenge: As seen from the north east- p.1
- Composite map of routes - p.4
- Artistic impression of a Neolithic house- p.5
- Illustration by Indigo Jones- p.8
- Barclay's plan of 1895 (Plan I)- p.9
- Barclay's vision of Stonehenge restored- p.10
- Sunset- p.11
- Illustration of the car park posts- p.12
- Newgrange: Ireland - p.14
- Newgrange seen from Knowth: Ireland- p.14
- Artistic view of the early henge along the 'solstice alignment'- p.15
- Artistic impression: The Great Cursus and Stonehenge seen to scale from above- p.16
- Stonehenge: North east elevation- p.17
- The Heel-stone's new position as seen from along the centre-line- p.18
- The Avenue: Barclay's extract from Stuckeley- p.19
- The Y and Z holes - p.20
- The outer perimeter of Avebury today - p.21
- Stones of the outer circle drawn from slightly off-centre - p.22

- A lintel of one of the trilithons - p.23
- Bluestones within the inner monument - p.24
- The fallen Slaughter-stone- p.25
- An example of the type of engraving found- p.29
- View of Stone 54 showing the 'T' shape - p.30
- Close-up on Stone 54- p.30
- Tracing stars using the North Pole - p.36
- The clock of the stars - p.37
- Following the stars - p.38
- Summer arrangement (angles)- p.39
- The World if a disc - p.40
- Haze in daytime- p.40
- Haze at sunrise- p.40
- Aligning to sunrise (tripods)- p.41
- Aligning to sunrise using tripods- p.41
- CGI image showing sea-horizon leveling- p.42
- A drawing of apparent geocentric movement of the sun- p.43
- Drawing the Universe (with England at the top of the world)- p.44
- The 56 divisions of the heavens from Southern England- p.45
- Modified & updated version of Stonehenge 1845 plan- p.45

INDEX

- The path of the setting sun - p.46
- Setting out the heavens at Salisbury - p.47
- The sun's orbits in a geocentric Universe - p.48
- Modified version of 1845 plan (unknown early centre)- p.49
- The Earth and solar markers- p.49
- Finding north- p.50
- The Avenue stones which were kept- p.51
- Computer generated image of Stonehenge grounds- p.51
- To trace the summer sun (on a geocentric world)- p.52
- An equatorial telescope at Herstmonceux- p.53
- Pole and stick arrangement to show the sun rotating- p.53
- Cast tin after cooling - p.54
- Cast tin after hand polishing- p.54
- Using mirrors to light up a model of a geocentric sun - p.54
- Adjusting the mirrors - p.55
- Using spherical mirrors to make a focal device - p.55
- The setting ring (winter mirrors)- p.56
- Summer: The sail pointing down - p.57
- High level position of the 3-season socket- p.58
- Raising the Maypole- p.58
- Setting the angle and location - p.59
- Stones 53 and 54- p.59
- The equinox support requirement- p.60
- The outer bluestone circle - p.60
- Oval or horse-shoe counterweight ring - p.61
- Stonehenge's inner bluestones - p.61
- The loading and rotation platforms- p.62
- Platforms for equinox and summer- p.63
- Rotation of the sail - p.63
- View from the north east - p.64
- Seeing the curvature of the Earth- p.68
- Using sticks as horizon sight-lines - p.68
- The highest hilltop ridge adjacent to Beachy Head - p.69
- The cliffs near Beachy Head - p.69
- Using a trough as a level - p.70
- Looking east from Beachy Head - p.70
- The hills to the north of Beachy Head - p.71
- Bourne Hill Tumulus - p.71
- Sight-lines (diagram)- p.72
- Raising a pole (diagram)- p.72
- The route from Beachy Head to Bourne Hill- p.73
- Foxholes Brow bowl tumulus- p.74
- View of Bourne Hill from Foxholes Brow- p.74
- Beachy Brow bowl tumulus- p.74
- View of Bourne Hill & Foxholes Brow from Beachy Brow- p.74
- Sighting on a flat bowl - p.75
- Location of other tumuli (near Eastbourne)- p.76
- After sunrise looking west- p.76
- Bourne Hill: Sunrise at equinox - p.77
- The angles to determine the size of the world (dagram)- p.77
- Combe Hill: Tumulus A - p.78
- Seeing the curvature of the Earth- p.79
- Combe Hill (adapted from Map by Curwen)- p.79
- Combe Hill: Showing how to calculate the curvature of the Earth- p.80
- Combe Hill: Bowl Tumulus B - p.80
- The route beyond Bourne Hill (Eastbourne)- p.81
- The Long Man, East Sussex - p.82
- The Long Man's Amphitheatre- p.82

- Following the rotation of the Heavens on a northern slope - p.83
- The stone correlated to Arthurian lore- p.86
- The stone correlated to Arthurian grail lore- p.87
- The stones and the Treasures of the Tuatha Dé Danann- p.88
- The Ptolemaic geocentric model of the Universe in 1568 - p.91
- The Copernican system by Andreas Cellarius - p.92
- A geocentric view: Extract from 'The Cosmographical Glasse'- p.93
- Stonehenge 1845 Ground plan with solstice lines shown- p.94
- Measuring at Stonehenge - p.98
- Stone 54- p.100
- The Last Supper- p.103
- Precession - p.107
- The Earth circling the Sun - p.108
- Movement of the Sun seen from the Equator - p.110
- Solar Planes; movement of the Sun seen at temperate latitudes- p.111
- The wheels of the sun- p.112
- Solar Azimuths: Extract from CIBSE Design Guide A- p.112
- Extract from US patent no 4170985 - p.114
- Ray reflection lines from a spherical mirror - p.115
- Zooming in to the half-radius point - p.115
- Spherical collection zones for a fixed mirror set- p.116
- Equinoctial solar sweeps of spherical mirrors - p.117
- Seasonal solar sweeps - p.117
- Ideal mirror zones for winter (6 month) period - p.118
- One of the early second stage proof tests (2008) - p.119
- Stage 3 and 4 tests- p.120
- The roller assembly - p.120
- Constructing the mirrors- p.120
- Focusing the mirrors- p.120
- Preliminary scheme drawing extracts (6 no)- p.121
- Fitting the model into Stonehenge- p.122
- Stone 54- p.122
- Stage 5 tests: 2013 - p.123
- Setting up the tests as Stonehenge- p.123
- Test frame 6: 2013 - p.124
- Test frame 6: 2013 - p.124
- Stage 6 tests: Willingdon in June 2013 - p.125
- Stage 6 tests: Stay ropes seen from below, June 2013 - p.125
- Stay-rope trajectory for lowest set of the pole - p.126
- Back-reflections: Stage 6 tests: Willingdon, June 2013 - p.126
- Notes: The winter founding point - p.134
- Notes: Winter solar angles- p.134
- Notes: Defining the rim- p.135
- Notes: Viewing angles- p.135
- Notes: Summer solar angles- p.136
- Notes: Effect on viewing angle of summer set-up- p.136
- Notes: Summary of mirror bowl rim height- p.137
- Notes: Intersection with the rim- p.137
- Notes: Vertical range of the end of the sail- p.137
- Notes: The three season device- p.138
- Notes: Timer-ring- p.138
- Notes: Locating where Salisbury and Stonehenge are positioned- p.140